The Master Plan of Evangelism presents a thorough examination of the Gospel accounts, revealing the objective of Christ's ministry and His strategy for carrying it out. Dr. Robert E. Coleman focuses on the underlying principles that consistently determined what His action would be in any given situation. By emulating His pattern, you'll be prepared to minister to the specific needs of those God brings into your life. This new edition includes a study guide by Dr. Roy Fish, which contains thirteen lessons for applying Christ's principles for evangelism. With the help of *The Master Plan of Evangelism,* you can be sure that your course of action fits into God's overall plan for the Great Commission. Every Christian who seeks to follow and witness for Jesus Christ should read this significant and relevant book.

Books by Robert E. Coleman

Established by the Word

Introducing the Prayer Cell

Life in the Living Word

The Master Plan of Evangelism

The Spirit and the Word

Dry Bones Can Live Again

One Divine Moment (Editor)

Written in Blood

Evangelism in Perspective

They Meet the Master

The Mind of the Master

Songs of Heaven

Growing in the Word

The New Covenant

The Heartbeat of Evangelism

Evangelism on the Cutting Edge (Editor)

The Master Plan of Discipleship

The Spark That Ignites

Nothing to Do but to Save Souls

The Great Commission Lifestyle

About the Author

Robert E. Coleman is Director of the School of World Mission and Evangelism and Professor of Evangelism at Trinity Evangelical Divinity School in Deerfield, Illinois. He also directs the Billy Graham Institute of Evangelism at Wheaton, Illinois, and is Dean of the Billy Graham International Schools of Evangelism. He is a graduate of Southwestern University in Texas, Asbury Theological Seminary, Princeton Theological Seminary, and has a Ph.D. from the University of Iowa.

Dr. Coleman is a founding member of the Lausanne Committee for World Evangelization and continues to serve on the United States Board. For 40 years he has been a pastor, evangelist, and educator. His ministry centers on life-style evangelism and discipleship, a concern reflected in all his writing. Twenty books have come from his pen, one or more of which have been translated and published in 85 languages, with English editions alone having a combined circulation of 4,500,000 copies.

THE MASTER PLAN of Evangelism

with study guide by Roy J. Fish

Robert E. Coleman

Fleming H. Revell Company
Tarrytown, New York

English Editions

First published, January, 1963
2nd Printing, November, 1964
3rd Printing, February, 1966
4th Printing, March, 1967
5th Printing, December, 1967
6th Printing, May, 1968
7th Printing, February, 1969
8th Printing, August, 1970
9th Printing, June, 1971
10th Printing, December, 1971
11th Printing, October, 1972
12th Printing, March, 1973
13th Printing, October, 1973
14th Printing, February, 1974
15th Printing, September, 1974
16th Printing, February, 1975
17th Printing, May, 1975
18th Printing, February, 1976
19th Printing, August, 1976
20th Printing, January, 1977
21st Printing, May, 1977
22nd Printing, December, 1977
23rd Printing, January, 1978
24th Printing, April, 1978
25th Printing, December, 1978
26th Printing, June, 1979
27th Printing, January, 1980
28th Printing, April, 1980
29th Printing, May, 1980
30th Printing, November, 1980

31st Printing, May, 1981
32nd Printing, December, 1982
33rd Printing, January, 1983
34th Printing, June, 1983
35th Printing, August, 1983
36th Printing, March, 1984
37th Printing, September, 1984
38th Printing, April, 1985
39th Printing, December, 1985
40th Printing, March, 1986
41st Printing, June, 1986
42nd Printing, September, 1986
43rd Printing, January, 1987
44th Printing, January, 1987
45th Printing, February, 1987
46th Printing, August, 1987
47th Printing, January, 1988
48th Printing, May, 1988
49th Printing, August, 1988
50th Printing, April, 1989
51st Printing, June, 1989
52nd Printing, November, 1989
53rd Printing, January, 1990
54th Printing, August, 1990
55th Printing, January, 1991
56th Printing, March, 1991
57th Printing, August, 1991
58th Printing, October, 1991
59th Printing, January, 1992
60th Printing, March, 1992

MORE THAN 1,000,000 COPIES IN PRINT IN ENGLISH EDITIONS.

Library of Congress Cataloging-in-Publication Data

Coleman, Robert Emerson, 1928—
    The master plan of evangelism.

    "Power books."
    Bibliography: p.
    1. Jesus Christ—Evangelistic methods.
I. Fish, R.J. II. Title.
BT 590.E8C6   1986   269'.2   86-13064
ISBN 0-8007-5229-5

Published by the Fleming H. Revell Company
Tarrytown, New York 10591
Printed in the United States of America

To
LYMAN and MARGARET
who dared to follow
the Master plan

CONTENTS

INTRODUCTION

Paul Stromberg Rees

"Philosophers," wrote Karl Marx, "have only *interpreted* the world differently; the point is, however, to *change* it."

However unlike they are in fundamental affirmations, the Christian Gospel and Communism are at this point in agreement. But the agreement goes little further. Distinctively, the Church proclaims the changed world as the consequence of changed men. Reflective man produces new philosophies; it is only regenerate man who holds the clue to a society that is really new.

It is this conviction, grounded in the Good News that "God was in Christ, reconciling the world unto Himself," that makes evangelism immensely more than a theory or a slogan. It brings it into focus as a necessity.

At this point, however, the question rises: How do we go forward with an evangelism—a widening of the circle of faith so that it includes more and more people who have transformingly trusted Christ as Saviour—that is continuous, contagious, and compelling?

Under the title *The Master Plan of Evangelism* Robert E. Coleman has presented a set of principles and sketched a scheme which, studied carefully, will go far toward rescuing the concept of evangelism from the realm of the "special" and the "occasional," and anchoring where it belongs in the essential, ongoing life and witness of the congregation.

There is nothing in the following pages that belittles what the Spirit of God has done, and continues to do, through the colossal, concerted, temporary undertakings of such evangelistic specialists as Moody, Sunday, or Graham. On the other hand, there is much that beckons us to the disciple-winning that works through small groups and builds toward congregational witness—all of it calculated to demonstrate the connection between the Gospel to which we bear testimony and the life which that Gospel enables us to live.

The author's work, concentrating as it does on the pattern we see in our Lord and His disciples, is saturated with Scripture. His style is unembellished. It is plain. It is direct. It unfailingly echoes the transparent sincerity of the mind that has thought long on the theme with which it is at grips.

Only this morning I heard a radio speaker make the observation that, in most matters, we move in either of two directions: from *words* to *things*, or from *things* to *words*. That is to say, if we do not make the journey from theories and ideals to concrete situations, then the concrete situations will be lost under a smog of words.

From the latter peril I believe this earnest volume can help deliver us. It is therefore a pleasure to commend it.

PREFACE

The Master and His Plan

THE PROBLEM IN EVANGELISTIC METHODS

Objective and relevance—these are the crucial issues of our work. Both are interrelated, and the measure by which they are made compatible will largely determine the significance of all our activity. Merely because we are busy, or even skilled, doing something does not necessarily mean that we are getting anything accomplished. The question must always be asked: Is it worth doing? And does it get the job done?

This is a question that should be posed continually in relation to the evangelistic activity of the church. Are our efforts to keep things going fulfilling the great commission of Christ? Do we see an ever-expanding company of dedicated men reaching the world with the Gospel as a result of our ministry? That we are busy in the church trying to work one program of evangelism after another can not be denied. But are we accomplishing our objective?

FORM FOLLOWS FUNCTION

Concern at this point immediately focuses the need for a well-thought-through strategy of movement day by day in terms of the long range goal. We must know how a course of action fits into the overall plan God has for our lives if it is to thrill our souls with a sense of destiny. This is true of any particular procedure or technique employed to propagate the Gospel. Just as a building is constructed according to the plan for its use, so everything we do must have a purpose. Otherwise our activity can be lost in aimlessness and confusion.

A STUDY IN PRINCIPLES

That is why this study has been attempted. It is an effort to see controlling principles governing the movements of the Master in the hope that our own labours might be conformed to a similar pattern. As such, the book does not seek to interpret specific methods of Jesus in personal or mass evangelism.[1] Rather this is a study in

1. There are a number of books which treat various phases of the evangelistic message and methodology of Jesus. Among those which provide many helpful insights are the following: Raymond Calkins, *How Jesus Dealt with Man* (Nashville: Abingdon-Cokesbury Press, 1942); Allan Knight Chalmers, *As He Passed By* (New York: The Abingdon Press, 1939); Ozora Davis, *Meeting the Master* (New York: Association Press, 1917); F. V. McFatridge, *The Personal Evangelism of Jesus* (Grand Rapids: Zondervan, 1939); G. Campbell Morgan, *The Great Physician* (New York: Fleming H. Revell Co., 1937); L. R. Scarborough, *How Jesus Won Men* (New York: George H. Doran Co., 1926); John Calhoun Sligh, *Christ's Way of Winning Souls* (Nashville: Publish-

principles underlying His ministry—principles which determined His methods. One might call it a study in His strategy of evangelism around which His life was orientated while He walked on the earth.

MORE RESEARCH NEEDED

There has been surprisingly little published along this line, though, of course, most books dealing with evangelistic methods will have something to say about it in passing. The same could be said for studies in Jesus' teaching methods,[1] as well as the general histories treating the life and work of Christ.[2]

---

ing House of the M. E. Church, South, 1909); John Smith, *The Magnetism of Christ* (London: Hodder and Stoughton, 1904); Mack Stokes, *The Evangelism of Jesus* (Nashville: Methodist Evangelistic Materials, 1960); Earnest Clyde Wareing, *The Evangelism of Jesus* (New York: The Abingdon Press, 1918); and Faris D. Whitesell, *Basic New Testament Evangelism* (Grand Rapids: Zondervan, 1949). In addition to these works which specifically treat evangelistic methods of Jesus, there are many more which give it particular attention in a chapter or two, such as R. W. Cooper, *Modern Evangelism* (New York: Fleming H. Revell, 1929), Chapter II; Charles G. Trumbull, *Taking Men Alive* (New York: Fleming H. Revell, 1927), Chapter IX; and S. A. Whitmer, *Galilean Fisherman* (Berne, Indiana: Life and Hope Publications, 1940), Chapter X. However, to a varying degree every work that treats the life or teachings of Christ will have some reference to His evangelistic methods, and many of these larger works will have the most complete discussion of individual cases to be found anywhere. Needless to say, there is no want of material in this field if one will only search it out.

1. A few of the more pertinent volumes and the pages relevant are: Walter Albeon Squires, *The Pedagogy of Jesus* (Philadelphia: Westminster, 1927), pp. 67–168; Norman E. Richardson, *The Christ of the Class Room* (New York: Macmillan, 1931), pp. 121–182; and J. M. Price, *Jesus the Teacher* (Nashville: Convention Press, 1954), pp. 31–60.

2. For example, helpful information relative to Jesus' strategy may be found in such well-known works as Samuel J. Andrews, *The*

Probably the most careful study to date in the Master's larger plan of evangelism has been done in reference to the training of the disciples, of which A. B. Bruce's *The Training of the Twelve* is the best.[1] First published in 1871 and revised in 1899, this narrative of the disciples' growth in the presence of the Master is still unsurpassed for wealth of insights into this subject. Another volume, *Pastor Pastorum* by Henry Latham, written in 1890, gives particular attention to Jesus' way of training men, though less comprehensive in its analysis.[2] Since the time of these earlier studies a number of other smaller volumes have appeared which offer helpful stimulus in pursuing this theme.[3] Not all of these works have the same

---

Life of Our Lord, reprint of 1891 ed. (Grand Rapids: Zondervan, 1954), pp. 121, 122; J. P. Lange, *The Life of the Lord Jesus Christ,* 4 vols., reprint (Grand Rapids: Zondervan, 1958), I, pp. 393–410; II, pp. 182–197; Alfred Edersheim, *The Life and Times of Jesus the Messiah,* 2 vols. (New York: E. R. Herrick & Co., 1886), I, pp. 472–477; David Smith, *The Days of His Flesh* (London: Hodder & Stoughton, 1905), pp. 157–167; and A. T. Robertson, *Epochs in the Life of Jesus* (New York: Charles Scribner's Sons, 1921), pp. 98–119.

1. A. B. Bruce, *The Training of the Twelve,* 3rd ed. (New York: Richard R. Smith, Inc., 1930).

2. Henry Latham, *Pastor Pastorum* (Cambridge: Deighton Bell and Co., 1910).

3. One almost hesitates to make a listing of these works since the degree of their significance to the thesis is so variable, and subject to interpretation, but at least the following selections that have come to my attention should be mentioned: Edwin A. Schell, *Traits of the Twelve* (Cincinnati: Jennings and Graham, 1911); Carl A. Glover, *With the Twelve* (Nashville: Cokesbury Press, 1939); F. Noel Palmer, *Christ's Way With People* (London: Marshall, Morgan & Scott, Ltd., 1943); and T. Ralph Morton, *The Twelve Together* (Glasgow: The Iona Community, 1956). Selected pages in other published works, to mention a few, are the chapters dealing with this subject in Alexander C. Purdy, *Jesus' Way With People* (New York: The Womans Press, 1926), pp.

evangelical theological viewpoint, but it is interesting to note that they come out at about the same place when it comes to evaluating the central thrust of Jesus' work with the disciples.

This is likewise true of numerous practical works on various phases of the Church life and ministry which have been published in recent years, most notably in the literature pertaining to the growing small group and lay witness movement in the church. While aware that these authors have not written primarily from the standpoint of evangelistic strategy, we must acknowledge our indebtedness to them for their reckoning of fundamental principles in the ministry and mission of our Lord.

However, the subject of Jesus' basic strategy has rarely been given the attention it deserves. Though we are appreciative of the labors of those who have considered it, and are not unmindful of their findings, the need for further investigation and clarification is always with us, and this is especially true of study within the primary sources themselves.

OUR PLAN OF STUDY

One has to go to the New Testament, and the Gospels in particular, to really see the plan of Jesus. They are after all the only eyewitness accounts that we have of the Master at work (Luke 1:2, 3; John 20:30; 21:24; I John 1:1). To be sure, the Gospels were written primarily to show us Christ, the Son of God, and that by faith we can have life in His name (John 20:31). But what sometimes we fail to realize is that the revelation

---

101–115; and Alexander Rattray Hay, *The New Testament Order for Church and Missionary* (Audubon, N.J.: New Testament Missionary Union, 1947), pp. 36–43.

of that life in Christ includes the way He lived and taught others so to live. We must remember that the witnesses who wrote the books not only saw the truth; they were changed by it. For this reason, in telling the story they invariably bring out those things which influenced them and others to leave all that they had to follow the Master. Not everything is reported, of course. Like any historical narrator, the Gospel writers paint a picture of the whole by elaborating upon a few characteristic persons and experiences, while bringing out certain critical points in the development of events. But of those things which are carefully selected and recorded in absolute integrity under the inspiration of the Holy Spirit, we can be sure that they are intended to teach us how to follow in the way of the Master. That is why the Scriptural accounts of Jesus constitute our best, and only inerrant, Textbook on Evangelism.

Hence the plan of this study has been to trace the steps of Christ as portrayed in the Gospels without undue recourse to secondary materials. In this pursuit, the inspired account of His life and work has been perused many times and from many angles trying to discern a motivating reason for the way He went about His mission. His tactics have been analyzed from the standpoint of His ministry as a whole, hoping thereby to see the larger meaning of His methods with men. Admittedly the task has not been easy, and I would be the first to acknowledge that there is more to learn. The boundless dimensions of the Lord of Glory simply cannot be confined within any human interpretation of His perfection, and the longer one looks at Him, the more he sees this to be the case.

CHRIST A PERFECT EXAMPLE

Yet recognizing this fact, there is no study more rewarding. Limited as our faculties of perception may be, we know that in the Master we have a perfect Teacher. He never made a mistake. Though partaking of our life, and being tempted in all points as we are, He was not bound by the limitations of the flesh which He accepted for our sake. Even when He did not choose to exercise His divine omniscience, His mind was clear. He always knew what was right, and as the perfect Man, He lived as God would live among men.

HIS OBJECTIVE WAS CLEAR

The days of His flesh were but the unfolding in time of the plan of God from the beginning. It was always before His mind. He intended to save out of the world a people for Himself and to build a church of the Spirit which would never perish. He had His sights on the day His Kingdom would come in glory and in power. This world was His by creation, but He did not seek to make it His permanent abiding place. His mansions were in the sky. He was going to prepare a place for His people that had foundations eternal in the heavens.

No one was excluded from His gracious purpose. His love was universal. Make no mistake about it. He was "the Saviour of the world" (John 4:42).[1] God wanted all men to be saved and to come to a knowledge of the truth. To that end Jesus gave Himself to provide a salva-

---

1. Scripture quotations, unless otherwise noted, are cited from the Standard American Revised Edition of the Bible, published in 1901.

tion from all sin for all men. In that He died for one, He died for all. Contrary to our superficial thinking, there never was a distinction in His mind between home and foreign missions. To Jesus it was all world evangelism.

HE PLANNED TO WIN

His life was ordered by His objective. Everything He did and said was a part of the whole pattern. It had significance because it contributed to the ultimate purpose of His life in redeeming the world for God. This was the motivating vision governing His behavior. His steps were ordered by it. Mark it well. Not for one moment did Jesus lose sight of His goal.

That is why it is so important to observe the way Jesus maneuvered to achieve His objective. The Master disclosed God's strategy of world conquest. He had confidence in the future precisely because He lived according to that plan in the present. There was nothing haphazard about His life—no wasted energy, not an idle word. He was on business for God (Luke 2:49). He lived, He died, and He rose again according to schedule. Like a general plotting His course of battle, the Son of God calculated to win. He could not afford to take a chance. Weighing every alternative and variable factor in human experience, He conceived a plan that would not fail.

WORTH CAREFUL CONSIDERATION

It is tremendously revealing to study it. Serious reflection at this point will bring the student of Christ to some profound and perhaps shattering conclusions, though the realization will likely be slow and arduous. In fact, at first glance it might even appear that Jesus had no plan.

Another approach might discover some particular technique but miss the underlying pattern of it all. This is one of the marvels of His strategy. It is so unassuming and silent that it is unnoticed by the hurried churchman. But when the realization of His controlling method finally dawns on the open mind of the disciple he will be amazed at its simplicity and wonder how he could have ever failed to see it before. Nevertheless, when His plan is reflected upon, the basic philosophy is so different from that of the modern church that its implications are nothing less than revolutionary.

The following pages attempt to clarify eight guiding principles of the Master's plan. However, it must be said that the steps are not to be understood as invariably coming in this sequence, as if the last were not initiated until the others had been mastered. Actually all of the steps were implied in each one, and in some degree they all began with the first. The outline is intended only to give structure to His method and to bring out the progressive logic of the plan. One will observe that as the ministry of Jesus Christ develops, the steps become more pronounced and the sequence more discernible.

1 · Selection

MEN WERE HIS METHOD

It all started by Jesus calling a few men to follow Him. This revealed immediately the direction His evangelistic strategy would take. His concern was not with programs to reach the multitudes, but with men whom the multitudes would follow. Remarkable as it may seem, Jesus started to gather these men before He ever organized an evangelistic campaign or even preached a sermon in public. Men were to be His method of winning the world to God.

The initial objective of Jesus' plan was to enlist men who could bear witness to His life and carry on His work after He returned to the Father. John and Andrew were the first to be invited as Jesus left the scene of the great revival of the Baptist at Bethany beyond the Jordan (John 1:35–40). Andrew in turn brought his brother Peter (John 1:41, 42). The next day Jesus found Philip on His way to Galilee, and Philip found Nathaniel (John 1:43–51). There is no evidence of haste in the selection of these disciples, just determination. James, the brother of John, is not mentioned as one of the group until the four fishermen are recalled several months later by the Sea of Galilee (Mark 1:19; Matt. 4:21). Shortly afterward Matthew is bidden to follow the Master as Jesus passed through Capernaum (Mark 2:13, 14; Matt. 9:9; Luke 5:27, 28). The particulars surrounding the call of the other disciples are not recorded in the Gospels, but it is believed that they all occurred in the first year of the Lord's ministry.[1]

As one might expect, these early efforts at soul winning had little or no immediate effect upon the religious life of His day, but that did not matter greatly. For as it turned out these few early converts of the Lord were destined to become the leaders of His church that was to go with the Gospel to the whole world, and from the standpoint of His ultimate purpose, the significance of their lives would be felt throughout eternity. That's the only thing that counts.

MEN WILLING TO LEARN

What is more revealing about these men is that at first they do not impress us as being key men. None of them occupied prominent places in the Synagogue, nor did any of them belong to the Levitical priesthood. For the most part they were common laboring men, probably having no professional training beyond the rudiments of knowledge necessary for their vocation. Perhaps a few of them came from families of some considerable means,

---

1. One qualification of an apostle mentioned in Acts 1:21, 22 was that he should have been with Jesus, "beginning from the baptism of John, unto the day that he was received up." Although this does not tell us from what point in John's baptismal work we are to reckon (certainly not at the beginning or from the Lord's own baptism), it does argue for an early association of all the apostles with Jesus, perhaps dating from the time of John the Baptist's imprisonment. See Samuel J. Andrews, *op. cit.*, p. 268; cf., Alfred Edersheim, *op. cit.*, I. p. 521.

such as the sons of Zebedee, but none of them could have been considered wealthy. They had no academic degrees in the arts and philosophies of their day. Like their Master, their formal education likely consisted only of the Synagogue schools. Most of them were raised in the poor section of the country around Galilee. Apparently the only one of the twelve who came from the more refined region of Judea was Judas Iscariot. By any standard of sophisticated culture then and now they would surely be considered as a rather ragged aggregation of souls. One might wonder how Jesus could ever use them. They were impulsive, temperamental, easily offended, and had all the prejudices of their environment. In short, these men selected by the Lord to be His assistants represented an average cross section of the lot of society in their day.[1] Not the kind of group one would expect to win the world for Christ.

Yet Jesus saw in these simple men the potential of leadership for the Kingdom. They were indeed "unlearned and ignorant" according to the world's standard (Acts

---

1. Many authors have sought to give us a picture of the twelve apostles. Among those which treat them all, in addition to those already cited in earlier footnotes, the following provide popular reading: George Matheson, *The Representative Men of the New Testament* (New York: Eaton & Mains, 1905); Edward Augustus George, *The Twelve* (New York: Fleming H. Revell, 1916); W. Mackintosh Mackay, *The Men Whom Jesus Made* (New York: George H. Doran Co., 1924); J. W. G. Ward, *The Master and the Twelve* (New York: George H. Doran Co., 1924); Charles R. Brown, *The Twelve* (New York: Harper, 1926); Francis Witherspoon, *The Glorious Company* (New York: Harcourt, Brace and Co., 1928); Asbury Smith, *The Twelve Christ Chose* (New York: Harper, 1958); William Barclay, *The Master's Men* (London: SCM Press, 1959); William Sanford LaSor, *Great Personalities of the New Testament* (Westwood, N.J.: Fleming H. Revell, 1961).

4:13), but they were teachable. Though often mistaken in their judgments and slow to comprehend spiritual things, they were honest men, willing to confess their need. Their mannerisms may have been awkward and their abilities limited, but with the exception of the traitor, their hearts were big. What is perhaps most significant about them was their sincere yearning for God and the realities of His life. The superficiality of the religious life about them had not obsessed their hope for the Messiah (John 1:41, 45, 49; 6:69). They were fed up with the hypocrisy of the ruling aristocracy. Some of them had already joined the revival movement of John the Baptist (John 1:35). These men were looking for someone to lead them in the way of salvation. Such men, pliable in the hands of the Master, could be molded into a new image—Jesus can use anyone who wants to be used.

CONCENTRATED UPON A FEW

In noting this fact, however, one does not want to miss the practical truth of how Jesus did it. Here is the wisdom of His method, and in observing it, we return again to the fundamental principle of concentration upon those He intended to use. One cannot transform a world except as individuals in the world are transformed, and individuals cannot be changed except as they are molded in the hands of the Master. The necessity is apparent not only to select a few laymen, but to keep the group small enough to be able to work effectively with them.

Hence, as the company of followers around Jesus increased, it became necessary by the middle of His second year of ministry to narrow the select company to a more manageable number. Accordingly Jesus "called His disciples, and He chose from them twelve, whom also He named apostles" (Luke 6:13–17; cf., Mark 3:13–19). Regardless of the symbolical meaning one prefers to put upon the number twelve,[1] it is clear that Jesus intended these men to have unique privileges and responsibilities in the Kingdom work.

This does not mean that Jesus' decision to have twelve apostles excluded others from following Him, for as we know, many more were numbered among His associates, and some of these became very effective workers in the Church. The seventy (Luke 10:1); Mark and Luke, the Gospel revelators; James, His own brother (I Cor. 15:7; Gal. 2:9, 12; cf., John 2:12 and 7:2–10), are notable examples of this. Nevertheless, we must acknowledge that there was a rapidly diminishing priority given to those outside the twelve.

---

1. Various opinions have been advanced as to why arbitrarily twelve disciples were designated apostles, for He could have selected more or gotten along with less, but probably the most plausible theory is that the number suggests a spiritual relationship of the apostolic company with the Messianic Kingdom of God. As Edwin Schell put it: "Twelve is the number of the spiritual Israel. Whether observed in the twelve patriarchs, in the twelve tribes, or in the twelve foundations of the twelve gates of the heavenly Jerusalem, the number twelve everywhere symbolizes the indwelling of God in the human family—the interpenetration of the world by divinity," Schell, *op. cit.*, p. 26; cf., Bruce, *op. cit.*, p. 32. It is altogether possible that the Apostles saw in the number a more literal meaning, and built up around it at first delusive hopes of the restoration of Israel in a political sense. They certainly were aware of their own place within the twelve, and were careful to fill up the vacancy created at the loss of Judas (Acts 1:15–26; cf., Matt. 19:28). One thing is certain, however, the number served to impress upon those chosen their importance in the future work of the Kingdom.

The same rule could be applied in reverse, for within the select apostolic group Peter, James, and John seemed to enjoy a more special relationship to the Master than did the other nine. Only these privileged few are invited into the sick room of Jairus's daughter (Mark 5:37; Luke 8:51); they alone go up with the Master and behold His glory on the Mount of Transfiguration (Mark 9:2; Matt. 17:1; Luke 9:28); and amid the olive trees of Gethsemane casting their ominous shadows in the light of the full Passover moon, these members of the inner circle waited nearest to their Lord while He prayed (Mark 14:33; Matt. 26:37). So noticeable is the preference given to these three that had it not been for the incarnation of selflessness in the Person of Christ, it could well have precipitated feelings of resentment on the part of the other apostles. The fact that there is no record of the disciples complaining about the preeminence of the three, though they did murmur about other things, is proof that where preference is shown in the right spirit and for the right reason offence need not arise.[1]

THE PRINCIPLE OBSERVED

All of this certainly impresses one with the deliberate way that Jesus proportioned His life to those He wanted to train. It also graphically illustrates a fundamental principle of teaching: that other things being equal, the more

1. Henry Latham suggests that the selection of these three served to impress upon the whole company the need for "self abnegation." In his analysis it actually was intended to show the apostles that "Christ gave what charge He would to whom He would; that in God's service it is honor enough to be employed at all; and that no man is to be discouraged because he sees allotted to another what appears to be a higher sphere of work than his own." Latham, op. cit., p. 325.

concentrated the size of the group being taught, the greater the opportunity for effective instruction.[1]

Jesus devoted most of His remaining life on earth to these few disciples. He literally staked His whole ministry upon them. The world could be indifferent toward Him and still not defeat His strategy. It even caused Him no great concern when His followers on the fringes of things gave up their allegiance when confronted with the true meaning of the Kingdom (John 6:66). But He could not bear to have His close disciples miss His purpose. They had to understand the truth and be sanctified by it (John 17:17), else all would be lost. Thus He prayed "not for the world," but for the few God gave Him "out of the world" (John 17:6, 9).[2] Everything depended upon their faithfulness if the world would believe on Him "through their word" (John 17:20).

NOT NEGLECTING THE MASSES

It would be wrong, however, to assume on the basis of what has here been emphasized that Jesus neglected the masses. Such was not the case. Jesus did all that any man could be asked to do and more to reach the multitudes. The first thing He did when He started His ministry was to identify Himself boldly with the great mass revival

---

1. The principle of concentration exemplified in the ministry of Jesus was not new with Him. It had always been God's strategy from the beginning. The Old Testament records how God selected a comparatively small nation of Israel through which to effect His redemptive purpose for mankind. Even within the nation, the leadership was concentrated usually within family lines, especially the Davidic branch of the tribe of Judah.

2. The high priestly prayer of Christ in the 17th chapter of John is especially meaningful in this connection. Of the 26 verses in the prayer, 14 relate immediately to the twelve disciples (John 17:6–19).

movement of His day through baptism at the hands of
John (Mark 1:9–11; Matt. 3:13–17; Luke 3:21, 22), and
He later went out of His way to praise this work of the
great prophet (Matt. 11:7–15; Luke 7:24–28). He Himself
continuously preached to the crowds that followed His
miracle-working ministry. He taught them. He fed them
when they were hungry. He healed their sick and cast out
demons among them. He blessed their children. Sometimes the whole day would be spent ministering to their
needs, even to the extent that He had "no leisure so much
as to eat" (Mark 6:31). In every way possible Jesus manifested to the masses of humanity a genuine concern. These
were the people that He came to save—He loved them,
wept over them, and finally died to save them from their
sin. No one could think that Jesus shirked mass evangelism.

MULTITUDES AROUSED

In fact, the ability of Jesus to impress the multitudes
created a serious problem in His ministry. He was so successful in expressing to them His compassion and power
that they once wanted "to take Him by force, to make
Him King" (John 6:15). One report by the followers of
John the Baptist said that "all men" were clamoring for
His attention (John 3:26). Even the Pharisees admitted
among themselves that the world had gone after Him
(John 12:19), and bitter as the admission must have been,
the chief priests concurred in this opinion (John 11:47,
48). However one looks at it, the Gospel record certainly
does not indicate that Jesus lacked any popular following
among the masses, despite their hesitating loyalty, and this
condition lasted right on down to the end. Indeed, it was

the fear of this friendly mass feeling for Jesus that prompted His accusers to capture Him in the absence of the people (Mark 12:12; Matt. 21:26; Luke 20:19).

Had Jesus given any encouragement to this popular sentiment among the masses, He easily could have had all the Kingdoms of men at His feet. All He had to do was to satisfy the temporal appetites and curiosities of the people by His supernatural power. Such was the temptation presented by Satan in the wilderness when Jesus was urged to turn stones into bread and to cast Himself down from a pinnacle of the temple that God might bear Him up (Matt. 4:1–7; Luke 4:1–4, 9–13). These spectacular things would surely have excited the applause of the crowd. Satan was not offering Jesus anything when he promised Him all the Kingdoms of the world if the Master would only worship him (Matt. 4:8–10). The arch deceiver of men knew full well that Jesus automatically would have this if He just turned His concentration from the things that mattered in the eternal Kingdom.[1]

But Jesus would not play to the galleries. Quite the contrary. Repeatedly He took special pains to allay the superficial popular support of the multitudes which had been occasioned by His extraordinary power (e.g., John 2:23–3:3; 6:26, 27). Frequently He would even ask those who were the recipients of His healing to say nothing

---

1. This is not intended to suggest that this was all that was involved in the temptation, but only to emphasize that the temptation appealed to the strategy of Jesus for world evangelism as well as to the spiritual purpose of His mission. Another interpretation of this temptation experience from the standpoint of evangelistic method, somewhat similar, is given by Colin W. Williams in his book, *Where in the World?* (New York: National Council of Churches of Christ), pp. 24–27.

about it in order to prevent mass demonstrations by the easily aroused multitudes.[1] Likewise, with the disciples following His transfiguration on the Mount "He charged them that they should tell no man what things they had seen" until after His resurrection (Mark 9:9; Matt. 17:9). On other occasions when applauded by the crowd, Jesus would slip away with His disciples and go elsewhere to continue His ministry.[2]

His practice in this respect sometimes rather annoyed His followers who did not understand His strategy. Even his own brothers and sisters, who yet did not believe on Him, urged Him to abandon this policy and make an open show of Himself to the world, but He refused to take their advice (John 7:2–9).

FEW SEEMED TO UNDERSTAND

In view of this policy, it is not surprising to note that few people were actually converted during the ministry of Christ, that is, in any clear-cut way. Of course, many of the multitudes believed in Christ in the sense that His divine ministry was acceptable,[3] but comparatively few seemed to have grasped the meaning of the Gospel. Perhaps His total number of devoted followers at the

1. Instances of this are the case of the cleansed leper (Mark 1:44, 45; Matt. 8:4; Luke 5:14–16); those freed from unclean spirits by the Sea of Galilee (Mark 3:11, 12); Jairus after seeing his daughter raised from the dead (Mark 5:42, 43; Luke 8:55, 56); the two blind men restored to sight (Matt. 9:30); and the blind man in Bethsaida (Mark 8:25, 26).

2. Some examples of this are in John 1:29–43; 6:14, 15; Mark 4:35, 36; 6:1, 45, 46; 7:24–8:30; Matt. 8:18, 23; 14:22, 23; 15:21, 39; 16:4; Luke 5:16; 8:22; and others.

3. Examples of this are John 2:23–25; 6:30–60; 7:31–44; 11:45, 46; 12:11, 17–19; Luke 14:25–35; 19:36–38; Matt. 21:8–11; 14–17; Mark 11:8–11.

end of His earthly ministry numbered little more than the 500 brethren to whom Jesus appeared after the resurrection (I Cor. 15:6), and only about 120 tarried in Jerusalem to receive the baptism of the Holy Spirit (Acts 1:15). Though this number is not small considering that His active ministry extended only over a period of three years, yet if at this point one were to measure the effectiveness of His evangelism by the number of His converts, Jesus doubtless would not be considered among the most productive mass evangelists of the church.

HIS STRATEGY

Why? Why did Jesus deliberately concentrate His life upon comparatively so few people? Had he not come to save the world? With the glowing announcement of John the Baptist ringing in the ears of multitudes, the Master easily could have had an immediate following of thousands if He wanted them. Why did He not then capitalize upon His opportunities to enlist a mighty army of believers to take the world by storm? Surely the Son of God could have adopted a more enticing program of mass recruitment. Is it not rather disappointing that one with all the powers of the universe at His command would live and die to save the world, yet in the end have only a few ragged disciples to show for His labors?

The answer to this question focuses at once the real purpose of His plan for evangelism. Jesus was not trying to impress the crowd, but to usher in a Kingdom. This meant that He needed men who could lead the multitudes. What good would it have been for His ultimate objective to arouse the masses to follow Him if these people had no subsequent supervision nor instruction in the Way? It had been demonstrated on numerous occasions that the crowd was an easy prey to false gods when left without proper care. The masses were like helpless sheep wandering aimlessly without a shepherd (Mark 6:34; Matt. 9:36; 14:14). They were willing to follow almost anyone that came along with some promise for their welfare, be it friend or foe. That was the tragedy of the hour—the noble aspirations of the people were easily excited by Jesus, but just as quickly thwarted by the deceitful religious authorities who controlled them. The spiritually blind leaders of Israel (John 8:44; 9:39–41; 12:40; cf., Matt. 23:1–39), though comparatively few in number,[1] completely dominated the affairs of the people. For this reason, unless Jesus' converts were given competent men of God to lead them on and protect them in the truth they would soon fall into confusion and despair, and the last state would be worse than the first. Thus, before the world could ever be permanently helped, men would have to be raised up who could lead the multitudes in the things of God.

---

1. The Pharisees and Sadducees were the principal leaders of Israel, outside of the ruling Roman forces, and the whole religious, social, educational, and to a limited degree, political life of the approximately 2,000,000 people in Palestine was molded by their action. Yet the number of persons belonging to the Pharisaic guild, composed mostly of rabbis and well-to-do lay folk, according to the estimate of Josephus (*Ant.*, XVII, 2, 4), did not exceed 6,000; while the total number of Sadducees, made up mostly of the chief priests and Sanhedrin families in Jerusalem, probably did not amount to more than a few hundred. See Anthony C. Deane, *The World Christ Knew* (London: Guild Books, 1944), pp. 57, 60; Edersheim, *op. cit.*, I, p. 311. When it is considered that this small privileged group of less than 7,000 people, representing about one-third of one percent of the population of Israel, guided the spiritual destiny of a nation, it is not difficult to see why Jesus spoke so much about them, while also teaching His disciples the strategic need for better leadership.

Jesus was a realist. He fully realized the fickleness of depraved human nature as well as the Satanic forces of this world amassed against humanity, and in this knowledge He based His evangelism on a plan that would meet the need. The multitudes of discordant and bewildered souls were potentially ready to follow Him, but Jesus individually could not possibly give them the personal care they needed. His only hope was to get men imbued with His life who would do it for Him. Hence, He concentrated Himself upon those who were to be the beginning of this leadership. Though He did what He could to help the multitudes, He had to devote Himself primarily to a few men, rather than the masses, in order that the masses could at last be saved. This was the genius of His strategy.

THE PRINCIPLE APPLIED TODAY

Yet, strangely enough, it is scarcely comprehended in practice today. Most of the evangelistic efforts of the church begin with the multitudes under the assumption that the church is qualified to conserve what good is done. The result is our spectacular emphasis upon numbers of converts, candidates for baptism, and more members for the church, with little or no genuine concern manifested toward the establishment of these souls in the love and power of God, let alone the preservation and continuation of the work.

Surely if the pattern of Jesus at this point means anything at all it teaches that the first duty of a pastor as well as the first concern of an evangelist is to see to it that a foundation is laid in the beginning upon which can be built an effective and continuing evangelistic ministry to the multitudes. This will require more concentration of time and talents upon fewer men in the church while not neglecting the passion for the world. It will mean raising up trained leadership "for the work of ministering" with the pastor (Ephesians 4:12).[1] A few people so dedicated in time will shake the world for God. Victory is never won by the multitudes.

Some might object to this principle when practiced by the Christian worker on the ground that favoritism is shown toward a select group in the church. But be that as it may, it is still the way that Jesus concentrated His

---

1. This idea is brought out clearly in the translation of Ephesians 4:11 and 12 in the *New English Bible*, which reads: "And these were His gifts: some to be apostles, some prophets, some evangelists, some pastors and teachers, to equip God's people for work in His service, to the building up of the body of Christ." Other modern versions bring out the same essential meaning, including the Weymouth, Phillips, Wuest, Berkeley, Williams, and the Amplified New Testament. The three clauses in verse 12 are made successively dependent upon the other, with the last being the climax. According to this interpretation, Christ gave a special gift to some officials in the Church for the purpose of perfecting the saints to do the service they have each to perform in the one great goal of building up Christ's body. The ministry of the Church is seen as a work involving all members of the body (compare I Cor. 12:18 and II Cor. 9:8). Luther brings out the same thing in his commentary on "Ephesians," as also does Weiss, Meier, DeWitte, and Salmond. For a good exposition of this verse from this point of view, see the volume on Ephesians in *The Expositor's Greek Testament* (Grand Rapids: Wm. B. Eerdmans Publishing Co.), pp. 330–331. Other views are ably presented by Abbott in "Ephesians and Colossians," *International Critical Commentary* (Edinburgh: T. T. Clark, 1897), pp. 119, 120; and Lange, "Galatians–Colossians," *Commentary on the Holy Scriptures* (Grand Rapids: Zondervan), pp. 150–151. A practical treatment of this overall idea may be found in Gaines S. Dobbins's book, *A Ministering Church* (Nashville: Broadman Press, 1960), Ch. II, "A Church Needs Many Ministers," pp. 15–29; and from still a different angle in Watchman Nee, *The Normal Christian Church Life* (Washington, D.C.: International Students Press, 1962).

life, and it is necessary if any permanent leadership is to
be trained. Where it is practiced out of a genuine love for
the whole church, and due concern is manifested toward
the needs of the people, objections can at least be recon-
ciled to the mission being accomplished. However, the
ultimate goal must be clear to the worker, and there can
be no hint of selfish partiality displayed in his relationships
to all. Everything that is done with the few is for the
salvation of the multitudes.

A MODERN DEMONSTRATION

This principle of selectivity and concentration is en-
graved in the universe, and will bring results no matter
who practices it, whether the church believes it or not. It
is surely not without significance that the Communists,
always alert to what works, adopted in a large measure
this method of the Lord as their own. Using it to their
own devious end they have multiplied from a handful of
zealots seventy-five years ago to a vast conspiracy of
followers that enslave nearly half the peoples of the world.
They have proved in our day what Jesus demonstrated so
clearly in His day that the multitudes can be won easily
if they are just given leaders to follow. Is not the spread
of this vicious Communistic philosophy, in some measure,
a judgment upon the church, not only upon our flabby
commitment to evangelism, but also upon the superficial
way that we have tried to go about it?

TIME FOR ACTION

It is time that the church realistically face the situation. Our days of trifling are running out. The evangelistic
program of the Church has bogged down on nearly every
front. What is worse, the great missionary thrust of the

Gospel into new frontiers has largely lost its power. In most lands the enfeebled church is not even keeping up with the exploding population. All the while the Satanic forces of this world are becoming more relentless and brazen in their attack. It is ironic when one stops to think about it. In an age when facilities for rapid communication of the Gospel are available to the Church as never before, we are actually accomplishing less in winning the world for God than before the invention of the horseless carriage.

Yet in appraising the tragic condition of affairs today, we must not become frantic in trying to reverse the trend overnight. Perhaps that has been our problem. In our concern to stem the tide, we have launched one crash program after another to reach the multitudes with the saving Word of God. But what we have failed to comprehend in our frustration is that the real problem is not with the masses—what they believe, how they are governed, whether they are fed a wholesome diet or not. All these things considered so vital are ultimately manipulated by others, and for this reason, before we can resolve the exploitation of the people we must get to those whom the people follow.

This, of course, puts a priority on winning and training those already in responsible positions of leadership. But if we can't begin at the top, then let us begin where we are and train a few of the lowly to become the great. And let us remember, too, that one does not have to have the prestige of the world in order to be greatly used in the Kingdom of God. Anyone who is willing to follow Christ can become a mighty influence upon the world providing, of course, this person has the proper training himself.

Here is where we must begin just like Jesus. It will be

slow, tedious, painful, and probably unnoticed by men at first, but the end result will be glorious, even if we don't live to see it. Seen this way, though, it becomes a big decision in the ministry. One must decide where he wants his ministry to count—in the momentary applause of popular recognition or in the reproduction of his life in a few chosen men who will carry on his work after he has gone. Really it is a question of which generation we are living for.

But we must go on. It is necessary now to see how Jesus trained His men to carry on His work. The whole pattern is part of the same method, and we cannot separate one phase from the other without destroying its effectiveness.

2 · Association

HE STAYED WITH THEM

Having called his men, Jesus made it a practice to be with them. This was the essence of His training program —just letting His disciples follow Him.

When one stops to think of it, this was an incredibly simple way of doing it. Jesus had no formal school, no seminaries, no outlined course of study, no periodic membership classes in which He enrolled His followers. None of these highly organized procedures considered so necessary today entered at all into His ministry. Amazing as it may seem, all Jesus did to teach these men His way was to draw them close to Himself. He was His own school and curriculum.

The natural informality of this teaching method of Jesus stood in striking contrast to the formal, almost scholastic procedures of the scribes. These religious teachers of His day insisted upon their disciples adhering strictly to certain rituals and formulas of knowledge, whereby they were distinguished from others; whereas Jesus asked only that His disciples follow Him. Knowledge was not communicated by the Master in terms of laws and dogmas, but in the living personality of One who walked among them. His disciples were distinguished,

not by outward conformity to certain rituals, but by being with Him, and thereby participating in His doctrine
(John 18:19).

TO KNOW WAS TO BE WITH

It was by virtue of this fellowship that the disciples
were permitted "to know the mysteries of the Kingdom
of God" (Luke 8:10). Knowledge was gained by association before it was understood by explanation. This was no
better expressed than when one of the band asked, "How
know we the way?" reflecting his frustration at the
thought of the Holy Trinity. Whereupon Jesus replied:
"I am the way, the truth, and the life" (John 14:5, 6),
which was to say that the point in question already was
answered, if the disciples would but open their eyes to the
spiritual reality incarnated in their midst.

This simple methodology was revealed from the beginning by the invitation that Jesus gave to those men whom
He wanted to lead. John and Andrew were invited to
"come and see" the place where Jesus stayed (John 1:39).
Nothing more was said, according to the Record. Yet
what more needed to be said? At home with Jesus they
could talk things over and there in private see intimately
into His nature and work. Philip was addressed in the
same essential manner, "Follow me" (John 1:43). Evi-
dently impressed by this simple approach, Philip invited
Nathaniel also to "come and see" the Master (John 1:46).
One living sermon is worth a hundred explanations. Later
when James, John, Peter, and Andrew were found mend-
ing their nets, Jesus reminded them in the same familiar
words, "Come ye after Me," only this time adding the
reason for it, "and I will make you fishers of men" (Mark
1:17; cf., Matt. 4:19; Luke 5:10). Likewise, Matthew was

called from the seat of custom with the same invitation, "Follow me" (Mark 2:14; Matt. 9:9; Luke 5:27).

THE PRINCIPLE OBSERVED

See the tremendous strategy of it. By responding to this initial call believers in effect enrolled themselves in the Master's school where their understanding could be enlarged and their faith established. There were certainly many things which these men did not understand—things which they themselves freely acknowledged as they walked with Him; but all these problems could be dealt with as they followed Jesus. In His presence they could learn all that they needed to know.

This principle which was implied from the start was given specific articulation later when Jesus chose from the larger group about Him the twelve "that they might be with Him" (Mark 3:14; cf., Luke 6:13). He added, of course, that He was going to send them forth "to preach, and to have authority to cast out devils," but often we fail to realize what came first. Jesus made it clear that before these men were "to preach" or "to cast out devils" they were to be "with Him." In fact, this personal appointment to be in constant association with Him was as much a part of their ordination commission as the authority to evangelize. Indeed, it was for the moment even more important, for it was the necessary preparation for the other.

CLOSER AS TRAINING ENDS

The determination with which Jesus sought to fulfill this commission is evident as one reads through the subsequent Gospel accounts. Contrary to what one might expect, as the ministry of Christ lengthened into the second and third years He gave increasingly more time to the chosen disciples, not less.[1]

Frequently He would take them with Him in a retreat to some mountainous area of the country where He was relatively unknown, seeking to avoid publicity as far as possible. They took trips together to Tyre and Sidon to the northwest (Mark 7:24; Matt. 15:21); to the "borders of Decapolis" (Mark 7:31; cf., Matt. 15:29) and "the parts of Dalmanutha" to the southeast of Galilee (Mark 8:10; cf., Matt. 15:39); and to the "villages of Caesarea Philippi" to the northeast (Mark 8:27; cf., Matt. 16:13). These journeys were made partly because of the opposition of the Pharisees and the hostility of Herod, but primarily because Jesus felt the need to get alone with His disciples. Later He spent several months with His disciples in Perea, east of the Jordan (Luke 13:22–19:28; John 10:40–11:54; Matt. 19:1–20:34; Mark 10:1–52). As opposition mounted there, Jesus "walked no more openly among the Jews, but departed thence into the country near to the wilderness, into a city called Ephraim; and there He tarried with His disciples" (John 11:54). When at last the time came for Him to go to Jerusalem, He significantly "took the twelve disciples apart" from the rest as He made His way slowly to the city (Matt. 20:17; cf., Mark 10:32).

In view of this, it is not surprising that during passion week Jesus scarcely ever let His disciples out of His sight.

---

1. Some scholars, like Henry Latham, have contended that prior to ordination of the apostles Jesus' first concern was with the multitudes, while afterward the emphasis shifted to the disciples, and especially to the Twelve. Henry Latham, *op. cit.*, pp. 188–269. Whether such a decisive division of concern is justified from the Record or not, the fact is clear that Jesus did increasingly give Himself to the apostolic company as time went on.

Even when He prayed alone in Gethsemane, His disciples were only a stone's throw away (Luke 22:41). Is not this the way it is with every family as the hour of departing draws near? Every minute is cherished because of the growing realization that such close association in the flesh soon will be no more. Words uttered under these circumstances are always more precious. Indeed, it was not until time began to close in that the disciples of Christ were prepared to grasp many of the deeper meanings of His presence with them (John 16:4). Doubtless this explains why the writers of the Gospels were constrained to devote so much of their attention to these last days. Fully half of all that is recorded about Jesus happened in the last months of His life, and most of this in the last week.

The course followed by Jesus through life was supremely portrayed in the days following His resurrection. Interestingly enough, every one of the ten post-resurrection appearances of Christ was to His followers, particularly the chosen apostles.[1] So far as the Bible shows, not a single unbelieving person was permitted to see the glorified Lord. Yet it is not so strange. There was no need to excite the multitudes with His spectacular revelation. What could they have done? But the disciples who had fled in despair following the crucifixion needed to be revived in their faith and confirmed in their mission to the world. His whole ministry evolved around them.

And so it was. The time which Jesus invested in these few disciples was so much more by comparison to that

1. This fact was impressively recognized by the disciples, as Peter said: "Him God raised up the third day, and gave Him to be made manifest, not to all the people, but unto witnesses that were chosen before of God, even to us who did eat and drink with Him after He rose from the dead" (Acts 10:40, 41).

given to others that it can only be regarded as a deliberate strategy. He actually spent more time with His disciples than with everybody else in the world put together. He ate with them, slept with them, and talked with them for the most part of His entire active ministry. They walked together along the lonely roads; they visited together in the crowded cities; they sailed and fished together in the Sea of Galilee; they prayed together in the deserts and in the mountains; and they worshipped together in the synagogues and in the Temple.

STILL MINISTERING TO THE MASSES

One must not overlook, too, that even while Jesus was ministering to others, the disciples were always there with Him. Whether He addressed the multitudes that pressed upon Him, conversed with the Scribes and Pharisees which sought to ensnare Him, or spoke to some lonely beggar along the road, the disciples were close at hand to observe and to listen. In this manner, Jesus' time was paying double dividends. Without neglecting His regular ministry to those in need, He maintained a constant ministry to His disciples by having them with Him. They were thus getting the benefit of everything He said and did to others plus their own personal explanation and counsel.

IT TAKES TIME

Such close and constant association, of course, meant virtually that Jesus had no time to call His own. Like little children clamoring for the attention of their father, the disciples were always under foot of the Master. Even the time He took to go apart to keep His personal devotions was subject to interruption at the disciples' need (Mark

6:46–48; cf., Luke 11:1). But Jesus would have it no other way. He wanted to be with them. They were His spiritual children (Mark 10:24; John 13:33; 21:5), and the only way that a father can properly raise a family is to be with them.

THE FOUNDATION OF FOLLOW-UP

Nothing is more obvious yet more neglected than the application of this principle. By its very nature, it does not call attention to itself, and one is prone to overlook the commonplace. Yet Jesus would not let His disciples miss it. During the last days of His journey, the Master especially felt it necessary to crystallize in their thinking what He had been doing. For example, once turning to those who had followed Him for three years, Jesus said: "Ye (shall) bear witness because ye have been with me from the beginning" (John 15:27). Without any fanfare and unnoticed by the world, Jesus was saying that He had been training men to be His witnesses after He had gone, and His method of doing it was simply by being "with them." Indeed, as He said on another occasion, it was because they had "continued with" Him in His temptations that they were appointed to be leaders in His eternal Kingdom where they would each eat and drink at His table, and sit on thrones judging the twelve tribes of Israel (Luke 22:28–30).

It would be wrong to assume, however, that this principle of personal follow-up was confined only to the apostolic band. Jesus concentrated Himself upon these few chosen men, but to a lesser and varying degree. He manifested the same concern with others that followed Him. For example, He went home with Zaccheus after his conversion on the street of Jericho (Luke 19:7), and He spent some time with him before leaving the city. After the conversion of the woman at the well in Samaria, Jesus tarried two extra days in Sychar to instruct the men of that community who "believed on Him because of the word of the woman who testified," and because of that personal association with them "many more believed," not because of the woman's witness, but because they heard for themselves the Master (John 4:39–42). Often one who received some help from the Master would be permitted to join the procession following Jesus, as for example, Bartimaeus (Mark 10:52; Matt. 20:34; Luke 18:43). In such a way many attached themselves to the apostolic company, as is evidenced by the seventy with Him in the later Judean ministry (Luke 10:1, 17). All of these believers received some personal attention, but it could not be compared to that given to the twelve.

Mention should be made, too, of that small group of faithful women who ministered to Him out of their substance, like Mary and Martha (Luke 10:38–42), Mary Magdalene, Joanna, Susanna, "and many others" (Luke 8:1–3). Some of these women were with Him to the end. He certainly did not refuse their gracious kindness, and often took the occasion to help them in their faith. Nevertheless, Jesus was well aware of the sex barrier, and although He welcomed their assistance, He did not try to incorporate these ladies into the select company of His chosen disciples. There are limitations in this kind of follow-up which one must recognize.

But apart from the rules of propriety, Jesus did not have the time to personally give all these people, men or women, constant attention. He did all that He could, and this doubtless served to impress upon His disciples the need for immediate personal care of new converts, but

He had to devote Himself primarily to the task of developing some men who in turn could give this kind of personal attention to others.

THE CHURCH AS A CONTINUING FELLOWSHIP

Really the whole problem of giving personal care to every believer is only resolved in a thorough understanding of the nature and mission of the church. It is well here to observe that the emergence of the church principle around Jesus, whereby one believer was brought into fellowship with all others, was the practice in a larger dimension of the same thing that He was doing with the twelve.[1] Actually it was the church that was the means of following up all those who followed Him. That is, the group of believers became the body of Christ, and as such ministered to each other individually and collectively.

Every member of the community of faith had a part to

---

1. One cannot help but observe in this connection that the references to "the disciples" as a corporate body are much more frequent in the Gospels than are references to an individual disciple. T. Ralph Morton even goes further with this analogy and contends that most of the references to individuals refer to failures on their part, while the references to the group as a whole more often speak of their joy, understanding, or achievement. When it is remembered that these accounts were written under inspiration by the disciples, and not Jesus, it is quite significant that they would set forth their own place in such terms. See T. Ralph Morton, op. cit., pp. 24–30, 103. We need not infer from this that the disciples were unimportant as individuals, for such was not the case, but it does impress us with the fact that the disciples understood their Lord to look upon them as a body of believers being trained together for a common mission. They saw themselves through Christ first as a church, and secondly as individuals within that body.

fulfill in this ministry. But this they could only do as they themselves were trained and inspired. As long as Jesus was with them in the flesh, He was the Leader, but thereafter, it was necessary for those in the church to assume this leadership. Again this meant that Jesus had to train them to do it, which involved His own constant personal association with a few chosen men.

OUR PROBLEM

When will the church learn this lesson? Preaching to the masses, although necessary, will never suffice in the work of preparing leaders for evangelism. Nor can occasional prayer meetings and training classes for Christian workers do this job. Building men is not that easy. It requires constant personal attention, much like a father gives to His children. This is something that no organization or class can ever do. Children are not raised by proxy. The example of Jesus would teach us that it can only be done by persons staying right with those they seek to lead.

The church obviously has failed at this point, and failed tragically. There is a lot of talk in the church about evangelism and Christian nurture, but little concern for personal association when it becomes evident that such work involves the sacrifice of personal indulgence. Of course, most churches insist on bringing new members through some kind of a confirmation class which usually meets an hour a week for a month or so. But the rest of the time the young convert has no contact at all with a definite Christian training program, except as he may attend the worship services of the church and the Sunday School. Unless the new Christian, if indeed he is saved, has parents or friends who will fill the gap in a real way, he is left entirely on his own to find the solutions to innumerable practical problems confronting his life, any one of which could mean disaster to his faith.

With such haphazard follow-up of believers, it is no wonder that about half of those who make professions and join the church eventually fall away or lose the glow of a Christian experience, and fewer still grow in sufficient knowledge and grace to be of any real service to the Kingdom. If Sunday services and membership training classes are all that a church has to develop young converts into mature disciples, then they are defeating their own purpose by contributing to a false security, and if the person follows the same lazy example, it may ultimately do more harm than good. There is simply no substitute for getting with people, and it is ridiculous to imagine that anything less, short of a miracle, can develop strong Christian leadership. After all, if Jesus, the Son of God, found it necessary to stay almost constantly with His few disciples for three years, and even one of them was lost, how can a church expect to do this job on an assembly line basis a few days out of the year?

THE PRINCIPLE APPLIED TODAY

Clearly the policy of Jesus at this point teaches us that whatever method of follow-up the church adopts, it must have as its basis a personal guardian concern for those entrusted to their care. To do otherwise is essentially to abandon new believers to the devil.

This means that some system must be found whereby every convert is given a Christian friend to follow until such time as he can lead another. The counselor should stay with the new believer as much as possible, studying the Bible and praying together, all the while answering questions, clarifying the truth, and seeking together to help others. If a church does not have such committed counselors willing to do this service, then it should be training some. And the only way they can be trained is by giving them a leader to follow.

This answers the question of how it is to be done, but it is necessary now to understand that this method can accomplish its purpose only when the followers practice what they learn. Hence, another basic principle in the Master's strategy must be understood.

3 · Consecration

HE REQUIRED OBEDIENCE

Jesus expected the men He was with to obey Him. They were not required to be smart, but they had to be loyal. This became the distinguishing mark by which they were known. They were called His "disciples" meaning that they were "learners" or "pupils" of the Master. It was not until much later that they started to be called "Christian" (Acts 11:26), although it was inevitable, for in time obedient followers invariably take on the character of their leader.

The simplicity of this approach is marvelous if not astounding. None of the disciples were asked at first to make a statement of faith or accept a well-defined creed, although they doubtless recognized Jesus to be the Messiah (John 1:41, 45, 49; Luke 5:8). For the moment all they were asked to do was to follow Jesus. Of course, clearly implied in their initial invitation was a call to faith in the Person of Christ and obedience to His Word. If this was not comprehended in the beginning, it would be perceived as they continued in the way with the Master. No one will follow a person in whom he has no trust, nor will he sincerely take the step of faith unless he is willing to obey what his leader says.

THE WAY OF THE CROSS

Following Jesus seemed easy enough at first, but that was because they had not followed Him very far. It soon became apparent that being a disciple of Christ involved far more than a joyful acceptance of the Messianic promise: it meant the surrender of one's whole life to the Master in absolute submission to His sovereignty. There could be no compromise. "No servant can serve two masters: for either he will hate the one, and love the other; or else he will hold to one, and despise the other. Ye cannot serve God and mammon" (Luke 16:13). There had to be a complete forsaking of sin. The old thought patterns, habits, and pleasures of the world had to be conformed to the new disciplines of the Kingdom of God (Matt. 5:1–7:29; Luke 6:20–49). Perfection of love was now the only standard of conduct (Matt. 5:48), and this love was to manifest itself in obedience to Christ (John 14:21, 23) expressed in devotion to those whom He died to save (Matt. 25:31–36). There was a cross in it—the willing denial of self for others (Mark 8:34–38; 10:32–45; Matt. 16:24–26; 20:17–28; Luke 9:23–25; John 12:25, 26; 13:1–20, et al.).

This was strong teaching. Not many of them could take it. They liked to be numbered among His followers when He filled their stomachs with bread and fish, but when Jesus started talking about the true spiritual quality of the Kingdom and the sacrifice necessary in achieving it (John 6:25–59), many of His disciples "went back, and walked no more with Him" (John 6:66). As they put it, "This is a hard saying: who can hear it?" (John 6:60). The surprising thing is that Jesus did not go running after them to try to get them to stay on His membership roll.

He was training leaders for the Kingdom, and if they were going to be fit vessels of service, they were going to have to pay the price.

MUST COUNT THE COST

Those who would not go all the way thus in time fell by the wayside. They separated themselves from the chosen company by reason of their own selfishness. Judas, exposed as a devil (John 6:70), held on until the end, but at last his greed caught up with him (Mark 14:10, 11, 43, 44; Matt. 26:14–16, 47–50; Luke 22:3–6, 47–49; John 18: 2–9). One simply could not follow Jesus through the course of His life without turning loose of the world, and those who made a pretense of it brought only anguish and tragedy to their souls (Matt. 27:3–10; Acts 1:18, 19).

Perhaps this is why Jesus spoke so severely to the scribe who came and said, "Master, I will follow Thee whithersoever Thou goest." Jesus frankly told this apparent volunteer for service that it would not be easy. "The foxes have holes and the birds of the air have nests; but the Son of Man hath not where to lay His head" (Matt. 8:19, 20; Luke 9:57, 58). Another disciple wanted to be excused from His immediate obligation of obedience in order that he might go and care for his aged father, but Jesus would allow no delay. "Follow Me," He said, "and leave the dead to bury the dead. Go thou and publish abroad the Kingdom of God" (Matt. 8:21, 22; Luke 9:59, 60). Another man indicated that He would follow Jesus, but on his own terms. He wanted to first bid farewell to his family, perhaps anticipating a merry good time doing it. But Jesus put it to him straight. "No man, having put his hand to the plough, and looking back is fit for the Kingdom of God" (Luke 9:62). Jesus did not have the time nor the desire to scatter Himself upon those who wanted to make their own terms of discipleship.

Hence it was that a would-be disciple was made to count the cost. "For which of you, desiring to build a tower, doth not first sit down and count the cost, whether he have wherewith to complete it?" (Luke 14:28). Not to do so was tantamount to inviting ridicule later from the world. The same would be true of a king in war who did not consider the cost of victory before hostilities began. To sum it up bluntly, Jesus said: "Therefore whosoever he be of you that renounceth not all that he hath, he cannot be my disciple" (Luke 14:33; cf., Mark 10:21; Matt. 19:21; Luke 18:22).

FEW WOULD PAY THE PRICE

Actually when the opportunists left Him at Capernaum because He would not satisfy their popular expectations, Jesus had only a handful of followers left. Turning to the twelve he said, "Would ye also go away?" (John 6:67). This was a crucial question. If these few men quit following Him, what would remain of His ministry? But Simon Peter answered, "Lord, to whom shall we go? Thou hast the words of eternal life. And we have believed and know that Thou art the Holy One of God" (John 6:68, 69). Indeed these words of the apostle must have been reassuring to the Master, for thereafter Jesus began to talk with His disciples more about His suffering and death, and with greater frankness.[1]

---

1. At least sixteen times prior to His actual arrest by the soldiers Jesus spoke of His suffering and death. His first references were veiled with mystery, but the implication was clear—the comparison of His body to the destruction of the temple (John 2:19); the reference to the Son of Man being lifted up like the brazen serpent

TO OBEY IS TO LEARN

This does not mean, however, that the disciples quickly understood everything the Lord said. Far from it. Their ability to grasp the deeper truths of the Lord's vicarious ministry was encumbered with all the limitations of human frailty. When Jesus told the disciples after the great affirmation at Caesarea Philippi that He would be put to death by the religious leaders in Jerusalem, Peter actually

---

(John 3:14); a remark concerning the day in which He as the bridegroom would be taken away (Mark 2:20; Matt. 9:15; Luke 5:35); the analogy of Himself with the bread of life which had to be broken and eaten (John 6:51–58); and possibly the reference to the prophet Jonah as a sign (Matt. 16:4). Following the bold affirmation of Peter at Caesarea Philippi, Jesus began to show unto His disciples more boldly "how that He must go unto Jerusalem, and suffer many things, and be rejected by the elders, and chief priests, and the scribes, and be killed, and after three days rise again" (Mark 8:31; Matt. 16:21; Luke 9:22). Thereafter He foretold His death and resurrection with detail while passing through Galilee with His disciples (Mark 9:30–32; Matt. 17:22, 23; Luke 9:43–45); and again on His last journey to Jerusalem after His ministry in Perea (Mark 10:33, 34; Matt. 20:18–19; Luke 18:32–33). His decease was the subject of His conversation with Moses and Elijah on the Mount of Transfiguration (Luke 9:31). It was also implied by His remark about a prophet not perishing out of Jerusalem (Luke 13:33), as well as the reference to the suffering and rejection of the people before His return in glory (Luke 17:25). He likened Himself to a Good Shepherd "who layeth down His life for the sheep" (John 10:11, 18), and as a grain of wheat that falls to the earth and dies before it could bring forth fruit (John 12:24). A few days before the last Passover Jesus again reminded His disciples that He would be "delivered up to be crucified" (Matt. 26:2), and later the same day He explained in the house of Simon the Leper that the precious ointment which Mary poured over His feet was in preparation for His burial (Mark 14:8; Matt. 26:12). Finally, at His last supper with His disciples Jesus told of His impending suffering (Luke 22:15), and then initiated the memorial of His death by eating bread and drinking wine (Mark 14:22–25; Matt. 26:26–29; Luke 22:17–20).

rebuked Him, saying, "Be it far from Thee, Lord: This shall never be unto Thee" (Matt. 16:22; cf., Mark 8:32). Whereupon Jesus had to tell the big fisherman that Satan deceived him at this point, "For thou mindest not the things of God, but of men" (Matt. 16:23; Mark 8:33). Nor did this end it. Again and again Jesus felt constrained to speak about His death, and its meaning to them, but it was not really comprehended until the day He was betrayed into the hands of His enemies.

Not comprehending clearly the message of the Cross, of course, they faltered at first in understanding their own place in the Kingdom. It was hard for them to accept the teaching of lowly servitude for the sake of others (Luke 22:24–30; John 13:1–20). They bickered among themselves who would be greatest in the Kingdom (Mark 9:33–37; Matt. 18:1–5; Luke 9:46–48). James and John wanted to have the prominent places (Mark 10:35–37; Matt. 20:20), and the other ten, displaying an envious spirit, were indignant about it (Mark 10:41; Matt. 20:24). They were unnecessarily harsh in their judgment upon others who did not agree with them (Luke 9:51–54). They were moved "with indignation" at parents who wanted Jesus to bless their children (Mark 10:13). Obviously, the practical outworking of what it meant to follow Christ was not fully experienced.

Yet Jesus patiently endured these human failings of His chosen disciples because in spite of all their shortcomings they were willing to follow Him. There was a brief interval of time after their initial call when they went back to their old fishing business (Mark 1:16; Matt. 4:18; Luke 5:2–5; cf., John 1:35–42), but their return does not seem to have been precipitated by any act of disobedience on their part. They just had not come to realize His purpose for their lives in leadership, or perhaps it had not yet been told them. Nonetheless, from the time that He appeared at their business and asked them to follow Him to become fishers of men, "they left all, and followed Him" (Luke 5:11; cf., Matt. 4:22, Mark 1:20). Later on, though they had much to learn, they could say that their dedication to Christ was still holding true (Mark 10:28; Matt. 19:27; Luke 18:28). With such men Jesus was willing to put up with a lot of those things which issued from their spiritual immaturity. He knew that they could master these defects as they grew in grace and knowledge. Their capacity to receive revelation would grow provided they continued to practice what truth they did understand.

Obedience to Christ thus was the very means by which those in His company learned more truth. He did not ask the disciples to follow what they did not know to be true, but no one could follow Him without learning what was true (John 7:17). Hence, Jesus did not urge His disciples to commit their lives to a doctrine, but to a Person Who was the doctrine, and only as they continued in His Word could they know the truth (John 8:31, 32).

THE PROOF OF LOVE

Supreme obedience was interpreted to be the expression of love. This lesson was underscored most emphatically on the eve of His death. As the disciples gathered around Him in the Upper Room following the Paschal meal, Jesus said: "If ye love Me, ye will keep my commandments . . . He that hath my commandments, and keepeth them, he it is that loveth Me; and he shall be loved of my Father, and I will love him, and will manifest myself unto him . . . If a man love Me, he will keep my word; and my father will love him, and we will come unto him and make our abode with him. He that loveth me not keepeth not my words; and the word which ye hear is not mine, but the Father's which sent Me. . . . If ye keep my commandments, ye shall abide in my love . . . This is my commandment, That ye love one another, as I have loved you. Ye are my friends if ye do whatsoever I have told you" (John 14:15, 21, 23, 24; 15:10, 12).

DEMONSTRATED BY JESUS

Absolute obedience to the will of God, of course, was the controlling principle of the Master's own life. In His human nature He continually gave consent to the will of His Father which made it possible for God to use His life fully according to its intended purpose. Repeatedly He sounded it out: "My meat is to do the will of Him that sent Me, and to accomplish His work (John 4:34); "I seek not My own will, but the will of Him that sent Me" (John 5:30; cf., 6:38); "I have kept my Father's commandments and abide in His love" (John 15:10; cf., 17:4). It could be summed up in His cry of Gethsemane, "Not My will, but Thine be done" (Luke 22:42; cf., Mark 14:36; Matt. 26:39, 42, 44).

The cross was but the crowning climax of Jesus' commitment to do the will of God. It forever showed that obedience could not be compromised—it was always a commitment unto death.

The worldly-minded religious leaders stated the truth when they said in derision: "He saved others; Himself He cannot save" (Mark 15:31; Matt. 27:42; Luke 23:35). Of course, He could not save Himself. He had not come to save Himself. He came to save the world. He came "not to be ministered unto, but to minister, and to give His life a ransom for many" (Mark 10:45; Matt. 20:28)

He came "to seek and to save that which was lost" (Luke 19:10). He came to offer Himself a sacrifice unto God for the sins of all men. He came to die. There was no other way that the inviolable law of God could be satisfied.

This cross, having already been accepted in advance (Rev. 13:8; cf., Acts 2:32), made each step that Christ took on the earth a conscious acceptance of God's eternal purpose for His life. When Jesus therefore spoke about obedience, it was something which the disciples could see incarnated in human form. As Jesus put it, "Ye should do as I have done unto you. Verily, verily, I say unto you, a servant is not greater than his Lord; neither he that is sent greater than He that sent him. If ye know these things, blessed are ye if ye do them" (John 13:15, 16). No one could miss this lesson. Just as Jesus found His blessedness in doing His Father's will, even so His followers would find theirs. This is the sole duty of a servant. It was true of Christ, and nothing less can ever be accepted as worthy of His disciple (Luke 17:6–10; cf., 8:21; Mark 3:35; Matt. 12:50).

THE PRINCIPLE IN FOCUS

From the standpoint of strategy, however, it was the only way that Jesus could mold their lives by His word. There could be no development of character or purpose in the disciples without it. A father must teach his children to obey him if he expects his children to be like him.

It must be remembered, too, that Jesus was making men to lead His church to conquest, and no one can ever be a leader until first he has learned to follow a leader. So He brought up His future commanders from the ranks, drilling in them along the way the necessity for discipline and respect for authority. There could be no insubordination in His command. No one knew better than Jesus that the Satanic forces of darkness against them were well organized and equipped to make ineffectual any half-hearted effort of evangelism. They could not possibly outwit the devilish powers of this world unless they gave strict adherence to Him who alone knew the strategy of victory. This required absolute obedience to the Master's will, even as it meant complete abandonment of their own.

THE PRINCIPLE APPLIED TODAY

We must learn this lesson again today. There can be no dilly-dallying around with the commands of Christ. We are engaged in warfare, the issues of which are life and death, and every day that we are indifferent to our responsibilities is a day lost to the cause of Christ. If we have learned even the most elemental truth of discipleship, we must know that we are called to be servants of our Lord and to obey His Word. It is not our duty to reason why He speaks as He does, but only to carry out His orders. Unless there is this dedication to all that we know He wants us to do now, however immature our understanding may be, it is doubtful if we will ever progress further in His life and mission. There is no place in the Kingdom for a slacker, for such an attitude not only precludes any growth in grace and knowledge, but also destroys any usefulness on the world battlefield of evangelism.

One must ask, why are so many professed Christians today stunted in their growth and ineffectual in their witness? Or to put the question in its larger context, why is the contemporary church so frustrated in its witness to the world? Is it not because among the clergy and laity alike there is a general indifference to the commands of God, or at least, a kind of contented complacency with mediocrity? Where is the obedience of the cross? Indeed, it would appear that the teachings of Christ upon self-denial and dedication have been replaced by a sort of respectable "do-as-you-please" philosophy of expediency.

The great tragedy is that little is being done to correct the situation, even by those who realize what is happening. Certainly the need of the hour is not for despair, but for action. It is high time that the requirements for membership in the church be interpreted and enforced in terms of true Christian discipleship. But this action alone will not be enough. Followers must have leaders, and this means that before much can be done with the church membership something will have to be done with the church officials. If this task seems to be too great, then we will have to start like Jesus did by getting with a few chosen ones and instilling into them the meaning of obedience.

It is when this principle is accepted in practice that we can develop fully according to the next step in the Master's strategy of conquest.

4 · Impartation

HE GAVE HIMSELF AWAY

Jesus wanted His followers to obey Him. But in recognizing this truth, He realized that His disciples would discover the deeper experience of His Spirit. And in receiving His Spirit they would know the love of God for a lost world. That is why His demands upon discipline were accepted without argument. The disciples understood that they were not just keeping a law, but were responding to One that loved them, and Who was willing to give of Himself for them.

His was a life of giving—giving away what the Father had given Him (John 15:15; 17:4, 8, 14). He gave them His peace by which He was sustained in tribulation (John 16:33; cf., Matt. 11:28). He gave them His joy in which He labored amid the sufferings and sorrows about Him (John 15:11; 17:13). He gave them the keys to His kingdom which the powers of Hell could never prevail against (Matt. 16:19; cf., Luke 12:32). Indeed, He gave them His own glory which was His before the worlds were made, that they all might be one even as He was one in the Father (John 17: 22, 24). He gave all He had—nothing was withheld, not even His own life.

Love is like that. It is always giving itself away. When

it is self-contained, it is not love. In this sense, Jesus brought clearly into focus before His followers just what was meant when "God so loved the world" (John 3:16). It meant that God gave all He had to those He loved, even His "only begotten Son." And for the Son, in incarnating that love, it meant renouncing His own right of living and giving His life for the world. Only in this light —when the Son is put in place of the world—can one even begin to understand the cross. Yet in this realization, the cross of Christ is inevitable, for the infinite love of God can only express itself in an infinite way. Just as man by his sin had to die, so God by His love had to send His Son to die in our place. "Greater love hath no man than this, that a man lay down his life for his friends" (John 15:13).

THE COMPULSION OF EVANGELISM

That is why He lost no opportunity to impress upon His followers the deep compulsion of His own soul aflame with the love of God for a lost world. Everything He did and said was motivated by this consuming passion. His life was simply the revelation in time of God's eternal purpose to save for Himself a people. Supremely this is what the disciples needed to learn, not in theory, but in practice.

And they say it practiced before them in many ways every day. Though the demonstrations were often painfully hard to accept, as when He washed their feet (John 13:1–20), they could not miss what He meant. They saw how their Master denied Himself many of the comforts and pleasures of the world and became a servant among them. They saw how the things which they cherished—

physical satisfaction, popular acclaim, prestige—He re-fused; while the things which they sought to escape—poverty, humiliation, sorrow, and even death—He ac-cepted willingly for their sake. As they watched Him minister to the sick, comfort the sorrowing, and preach the Gospel to the poor, it was clear that the Master con-sidered no service too small nor sacrifice too great when it was rendered for the glory of God. They may not have always understood it, and certainly could not explain it, but they could never mistake it.

HIS SANCTIFICATION

The constant renewing of His consecration of Himself to God through loving service to others constituted Jesus' sanctification. This was brought out clearly in His High Priestly prayer when he said: "As Thou didst send Me into the world, even so sent I them into the world. And for their sakes I sanctify Myself, that they themselves also may be sanctified in truth" (John 17:18, 19). Note that this setting apart of Himself unto God, which is indicated in the word "sanctify," was not necessary in Jesus' case to effect cleansing, since He was always pure. Nor was it necesary in order to receive power for service, since Jesus already had all the power He could use. Rather His sanctification, as the context reveals, was in the area of commitment to the task for which He had been "sent into the world,"[1] and in dedication to that purpose of evan-gelism, He continually gave His life "for their sakes."

His sanctification then was not for the purpose of bene-

---

1. Sanctification is used also in reference to Jesus in John 10:36, where again the idea is basically evangelistic in application.

fiting Himself, but it was for His disciples, that they might "be sanctified in truth."[1] That is to say, in giving Himself to God, Jesus gave Himself to those about Him so that they might come to know through His life a similar commitment to the mission for which He had come into the world. His whole evangelistic plan hinged on this dedication, and in turn, the faithfulness with which His disciples gave themselves in love to the world about them.

CREDENTIALS OF THE MINISTRY

This was to be the measure by which they were to regard their own service in His Name. They were to give as freely as they had received (Matt. 10:8). They were to love one another as He loved them (John 13:34, 35). By this token they were to be His disciples (John 15:9,

---

1. The tenses of the word "sanctify" reveal one important difference between the sanctification of Jesus and that of His disciples. The word for the Master's sanctification is in the present indicative, indicating a continuous condition—"I continue to sancitify Myself." On the other hand, when Jesus refers to His disciples in the next phrase, the perfect passive participle is used with the word "to be," making a paraphrastic construction which means here that there is a definite crisis of commitment in the sanctification of the disciples, though the emphasis is still largely upon the continuing result of that crisis. An expanded free interpretation of this passage in John 17:19 might read thus: "For their sakes I continually—moment by moment—renew my commitment to the work of evangelism, and I am willing to make every sacrifice necessary to accomplish this purpose of God for My life. And because I know that nothing else will suffice if the work of God is to be carried on in the future, I am asking the same of you. I have appointed you to go out and do My work, but before you will really feel My compassion for the lost world, you will have to make a full commitment of all that you are and all that you have to God's plan of world evangelism, and keep it up every day of your lives." I believe that such a dedication taken to heart would do more for the evangelization of the world than anything else. Surely it is a dimension of the sanctified life that needs more emphasis.

10). Herein was contained all His commandments (John 15:12, 17; cf., Matt. 22:37–40; Mark 12:30, 31; Luke 10:27). Love—Calvary love—was the standard. Just as they had seen for three years, the disciples were to give themselves in selfless devotion to those whom the Father loved and for whom their Master died (John 17:23).

Such a demonstration of love through them was to be the way that the world would know that the Gospel was true. How else would the multitudes ever be convinced? Love is the only way to win the free response of men, and this is possible only by the Presence of Christ within the heart. Thus Jesus prayed: "O righteous Father, the world knew Thee not, but I knew Thee; and these knew that Thou didst send Me; and I made known unto them Thy Name, and will make it known; that the love wherewith Thou lovedst Me may be in them, and I in them" (John 17:25, 26).

THE WORK OF THE HOLY SPIRIT

Let no one imagine, however, that this kind of an experience with Christ could be engendered by human ingenuity. Jesus made it abundantly clear that His life was mediated only through the Holy Spirit. "It is the Spirit that quickeneth; the flesh profiteth nothing" (John 6:63). That is why even to begin to live in Christ one had to be born again (John 3:3–9). The corrupted nature of man had to be regenerated by the Spirit of God before it could be conformed to its true created purpose in the Divine image. Likewise, it was the Spirit that sustained and nourished the transformed life of a disciple as he continued to grow in knowledge and grace (John 4:14; 7:38, 39). By the same Spirit one was made clean through the Word and set apart unto God for holy service (John 15:3;

17:17; cf., Eph. 5:26). From beginning to end, experiencing the living Christ in any personal way was the work of the Holy Spirit.

By the same token it was only the Spirit of God that enabled one to carry on the redemptive mission of evangelism. Jesus underscored this truth early in relation to His own work by declaring that what He did was in cooperation with "the Spirit of the Lord." It was by His virtue that He preached the Gospel to the poor, healed the brokenhearted, proclaimed deliverance to the captive, opened the eyes of the blind, cast out demons, and set at liberty those that were oppressed (Luke 4:18; Matt. 12:28). Jesus was God in revelation; but the Spirit was God in operation. He was the Agent of God actually effecting through men the eternal plan of salvation. Thus Jesus explained to His disciples that the Spirit would prepare the way for their ministry. He would give them utterance to speak (Matt. 10:19, 20; Mark 13:11; Luke 12:12). He would convict the world "in respect of sin, and of righteousness, and of judgment" (John 16:9). He would give illumination of truth that men might know the Lord (Matt. 22:43; cf., Mark 12:36; John 16:14). By His power the disciples were promised the very ability to do the works of their Lord (John 14:12).[1] In this light, evan-

---

1. This verse in John 14:12 has an application to evangelism that is staggering to comprehend, for not only does it say that the disciples will do the works of Christ, but it also says that they will do "greater works" because Jesus was going to the Father. Taken as it stands, this passage would teach us that the disciples in the power of the Holy Spirit were to do everything which their Lord had done—and that takes in quite a bit—and yet do even more. As to what these greater deeds were to be, Jesus did not say, but from the Acts of the Apostles it would obviously be in the realm of evangelism. At least, in this respect, the disciples actually did see

gelism was not interpreted as a human undertaking at all, but a divine project which had been going on from the beginning and would continue until God's purpose was fulfilled. It was altogether the Spirit's work. All the disciples were asked to do was to let the Spirit have complete charge of their lives.

ANOTHER COMFORTER

From the standpoint of their own satisfaction, however, the disciples needed to learn in a more meaningful way the relationship of the Spirit to the Person of their Lord. Jesus, of course, recognized this need, and therefore He spoke more specifically about it as the days of His flesh came to a close. Up to this point He had always been with them. He had been their Comforter; their Teacher; their Guide. In fellowship with Him the disciples had known courage and strength; with Him they felt that everything was possible; but their trouble was that Jesus was going back to Heaven. Under these circumstances, Jesus needed to explain to them how they would get along after He had gone.

It was at this time that Jesus told them about the Spirit as "Another Comforter,"[1] an Advocate, One Who

---

more results than Christ. In fact, just in one day at Pentecost more people were added to the church than had been accumulated during the three years of Jesus' ministry.

1. The word "Another" here is of a peculiar significance in the original Greek. It is not the word used to compare two objects of a dissimilar quality, but rather the word used to compare two things of the same essential quality, there being a difference only in person. Hence the value of this word is that it identifies the quality of the Spirit with that of the incarnate Son, so that the Spirit, while different in Person, is exactly like Jesus in His ministry to the disciples. See G. Campbell Morgan, *The Teaching of Christ* (New York: Revell, 1913), p. 65. Excellent treatment of

would stand by their side, a Person that would take exactly the same place with them in the unseen realm of reality that Jesus had filled in the visible experience of the flesh (John 14:16). Just as He had ministered to them for three years, now the Spirit would guide them into all truth (John 16:13). He would show them things to come (John 16:13). He would teach them what they needed to know (John 14:26). He would help them pray (John 14:12, 13; 16:23, 24). In short, He would glorify the Son by taking the things of Christ and making them real to His followers (John 16:14, 15). The world could not receive this truth, for it did not know Jesus; but the disciples knew Him, for He was with them, and in the Spirit, He would continue to be with them forever (John 14:17).

This **was** no theory, no creed, no makeshift arrangement that Jesus was talking about. It was the promise of a real compensation for the loss which the disciples were to sustain. "Another Comforter" just like Jesus was to fill them with the very Presence of the Master. Indeed, the privileges which the disciples were to enjoy in this deeper relationship to the Spirit were greater than they had known as Jesus walked with them along the roads of Galilee. After all, in His flesh, Jesus was confined to one body and one place, but in the Spirit these limitations were all removed. Now He could be with them always, and literally be enabled never to leave them nor forsake them (Matt. 28:20; cf., John 14:16). Looking at it from this perspective, it was better for Jesus, having finished His

Jesus' teaching about the Spirit's work may be found in Louis Burton Crane, *The Teaching of Jesus Concerning the Holy Spirit* (New York: American Tract Society, 1905); and J. Ritchie Smith, *The Holy Spirit in the Gospels* (New York: Macmillan, 1926).

work, to return to the Father and send the blessed Comforter to come and take His place (John 16:7).

THE SECRET OF THE VICTORIOUS LIFE

It is easy to see then why Jesus expected His disciples to tarry until this promise became a reality to them (Luke 24:49; Acts 1:4, 5, 8; 2:33). How else could they ever fulfill the commission of their Lord with joy and inward peace? They needed an experience of Christ so real that their lives would be filled with His Presence. Evangelism had to become a burning compulsion within them purifying their desires and guiding their thoughts. Nothing less than a personal baptism of the Holy Spirit would suffice. The superhuman work to which they were called demanded supernatural help—an enduement of power from on High. This meant that the disciples through confession of their deep-seated pride and enmity in utter surrender of themselves to Christ had to come by faith into a new and refining experience of the Spirit's infilling.[1]

---

1. This promise was fulfilled to the disciples at Pentecost (Acts 2:4). However, it was not ended there. Repeatedly Luke calls to our attention that the infilling of the Holy Spirit was the abiding and sustaining experience of the early Church (Acts 4:8, 31; 6:3, 5; 7:55; 9:17; 11:24; 13:9, 52). Certainly from this it would appear that the Spirit-filled life was accepted as the norm of Christian experience, although it was not a reality to all. This is why, for example, Paul was constrained to exhort the Ephesians to "be filled with the Holy Spirit" (Ephesians 5:18). In this connection, it would be good to read William Arthur, *The Tongue of Fire* (London: The Epworth Press, 1956); John Wesley, *A Plain Account of Christian Perfection* (London: Epworth Press, n.d.); Samuel Chadwick, *The Way to Pentecost* (New York: Fleming H. Revell, 1932); Charles G. Finney, "Be Filled with the Spirit," in *Revival Lectures* (New York: Fleming H. Revell, 1958); Andrew Murray, *The Full Blessing of Pentecost* (London: Oliphants Ltd., 1954); Samuel Logan Brengle, *When the Holy Ghost Is*

The fact that these men were of the common lot of mankind was no hindrance at all. It only serves to remind us of the mighty power of the Spirit of God accomplishing His purpose in men fully yielded to His control. After all, the power is in the Spirit of Christ. It is not who we are, but Who He is that makes the difference.

A TRUTH HIDDEN FROM UNBELIEVERS

However, it is well to mention again that only those who followed Jesus all the way came to know the glory of this experience. Those who followed at a distance, like the multitudes, as well as those who stubbornly refused to walk in the light of His Word, like the Pharisees, did not even hear about the work of the blessed Comforter. As noted before, Jesus would not cast His pearls before those who did not want them.[1]

Come (New York: Salvation Army Printing and Publishing House, 1911); R. A. Torrey, *The Baptism With the Holy Spirit* (New York: Fleming H. Revell, 1895); V. R. Edman, *They Found the Secret* (Grand Rapids: Zondervan, 1960); and the sermon "How to be Filled with the Holy Spirit" by Billy Graham, *Revival in Our Time* (Wheaton: VanKampen, 1950), just to mention a few of the more popular presentations of this subject. Terminology used in describing this experience may vary depending upon one's particular theological perspective, but a study of Christian history will reveal that the reality of the experience itself, howsoever it may be defined, is common to those who have been greatly used of God in making the Gospel relevant to others.

1. A good example of this is the famous Sermon on the Mount (Matt. 5:3–7:27; Luke 6:20–49). It was not addressed primarily to the wayfaring crowd, although they overheard it (Matt. 7:28, 29). Rather this sublime statement concerning the moral and ethical conduct of the Kingdom was delivered to those few close followers who could appreciate it. "Seeing this multitude, He went up into the mountain; and when He was set down, His disciples came unto Him, and He opened His mouth and taught them" (Matt. 5:1, 2; cf., Luke 6:17–20). Perhaps the most striking illustration of

This characterized His teaching throughout life. Jesus purposely reserved for His few chosen disciples, and particularly the twelve, His most revealing things (Luke 10:22; Matt. 11:27; cf., 16:17). Indeed, their eyes and ears were blessed. Many prophets and kings had desired to see the things which they saw, and to hear the things which they heard, yet could not (Matt. 13:16, 17; Luke 10:23, 24; cf., Matt. 13:10, 11; Mark 4:10, 11; Luke 8:9, 10). Such a policy may seem strange until it is realized again that Jesus was deliberately investing all He had in these few men so that they could be properly prepared to do His work.

THE PRINCIPAL ISSUE TODAY

The whole thing evolves around the Person of the Master. Basically His way was His life. And so it must be with His followers. We must have His life in us by the Spirit if we are to do His work and practice His teaching. Any evangelistic work without this is as lifeless as it is meaningless. Only as the Spirit of Christ in us exalts the Son are men drawn unto the Father.

Of course, we cannot give something away which we do not possess ourselves. The very ability to give away our life in Christ is the proof of its possession. Nor can we withhold that which we possess in the Spirit of Christ,

---

the deliberate way that Jesus withheld teaching from those who did not want it is the way He guarded His own association with the Messianic Promise. Although He made this claim to His friends early in His ministry (John 4:25, 26, 42), and allowed His disciples to affirm it from the beginning (John 1:41, 45, 49), there is no record that He ever declared that He was the Messiah to the religious rulers of Jerusalem until He was on trial, and then only after the high priest asked Him point-blank if He was the Christ (Mark 14:61, 62; Matt. 26:63, 64).

and still keep it. The Spirit of God always insists on making Christ known. Here is the great paradox of life— we must die to ourselves in order to live in Christ, and in that renunciation of ourselves, we must give ourselves away in service and devotion to our Lord. This was Jesus' method of evangelism, seen at first only by His few followers, but through them it was to become the power of God in overcoming the world.

But we cannot stop there. It is also necessary for one to see in us a clear demonstration of the way to live His life. Thus, we must understand another obvious aspect of Jesus' strategy with His disciples.

5 · Demonstration

HE SHOWED THEM HOW TO LIVE

Jesus saw to it that His disciples learned His way of living with God and man. He recognized that it was not enough just to get people into His spiritual communion. His disciples needed to know how His experience was to be maintained and shared if it was to be perpetuated in evangelism. Of course, in a technical sense, life precedes action, but in a thoroughly practical point of view, we live by what we do. One must breathe, eat, exercise, and carry on work normally if he is to grow. Where these functions of the body are neglected, life will cease to be. That is why the effort of Jesus to get across to His followers the secrets of His spiritual influence needs to be considered as a deliberate course of His master strategy. He knew what was important.

THE PRACTICE OF PRAYER

Take, for example, His prayer life. Surely it was no accident that Jesus often let His disciples see Him conversing with the Father.[1] They could see the strength which it

---

[1] More than twenty times the Gospels call attention to Jesus' practice of prayer. It is given special mention during events of

gave to His life, and though they could not understand fully what it was all about, they must have realized that this was part of His secret of life. Note that Jesus did not force the lesson upon them, but rather He just kept praying until at last the disciples got so hungry that they asked Him to teach them what He was doing.

Seizing His opportunity when it did come, Jesus proceeded to give them a lesson which their hearts were prepared to receive. He explained to them some of the more basic principles of prayer, and then before He finished, He illustrated what He meant by repeating before them a model prayer (Luke 11:1–11; Matt. 6:9–13). One might possibly think that such a practice was below the capabilities of these disciples—the idea of having to put words

momentous decision in His life—His baptism (Luke 3:21); the selection of the twelve apostles (Luke 6:12); on the Mount of Transfiguration (Luke 9:29); the Last Supper (Matt. 26:27); in Gethsemane (Luke 22:39–46); and on the cross (Luke 23:46). The Revelators also were impressed to record their Lord's intercession in connection with their own ministry—the confession of His Messiahship (Luke 9:18); on hearing their reports of evangelism (Luke 10:21, 22); teaching them to pray (Luke 11:1); the great high priestly prayer before He goes to die (John 17:6–19); the loving concern for Peter (Luke 22:32); and at the home of the two disciples in Emmaus after the resurrection (Luke 24:30). Prayer is prominent also in the exercise of His power-working miracles—healing the multitudes (Mark 1:35); feeding the five thousand (Mark 6:41; Matt. 14:19; Luke 9:16; John 6:11); later feeding the four thousand (Mark 8:6; Matt. 15:36); healing the deafmute (Mark 7:34); and raising Lazarus from the dead (John 11:41). Moreover, prayer is on the lips of Jesus as He looks at the multitudes whom He came to save—before conflict with religious leaders (Luke 5:16); in the discussion with the Greeks who came to see Him (John 12:27); after sending away the five thousand who had been fed (Mark 6:46; Matt. 14:23); blessing little children (Mark 10:16); and finally for those who nailed Him to the cross (Luke 23:34).

in their mouths to get them to pray—but Jesus would not take such an important matter as this for granted. Indeed, such elementary methods of teaching are often necessary to get people started in this discipline. But whatever it took, Jesus was determined to get this lesson across.

Thereafter He emphasized the life of prayer again and again when talking with His disciples, continually enlarging upon its meaning and application as they were able to comprehend deeper realities of His Spirit. It was an indispensable part of their training, which in turn they would have to transmit to others. One thing is certain. Unless they grasped the meaning of prayer, and learned how to practice it with consistency, not much would ever come from their lives.

USING SCRIPTURE

Another aspect of Jesus' life which was vividly portrayed to the disciples was the importance and use of the Holy Scriptures.[1] This was evident both in maintaining

1. There was never any confusion in His mind respecting their credibility and witness, for He knew that they were inspired by the Holy Spirit (Mark 12:36; Matt. 22:43). The written Scriptures were for Him "the Word of God" (John 10:35; Mark 7:13; Matt. 15:6; cf., Luke 8:12). Indeed, in a unique sense, they were His own Word which He interpreted and deepened (e.g., Matt. 5:21, 22, 27, 28), as He declared, "These are they which bear witness of Me" (John 5:39; cf., Matt. 5:17, 18). In this consciousness, He full well realized that His life was the fulfillment of Scripture, and frequently He called attention to that fact (Matt. 5:18; 8:17; 13:14; 26:54, 56; Mark 14:49; Luke 4:21; 21:22; John 13:18; 15:25; 17:12). It is only natural, then, that Jesus utilized this ready source of sure knowledge in His work. This was the food which nourished His soul (Matt 4:4) and fortified His heart against temptation (Matt. 4:4, 7, 10; 12:3; Luke 4:4, 8, 12). But above all, it was His Textbook for teaching in public and private the eternal truth of God (e.g., Luke 4:17–21; 24:27, 32, 44, 45).

His own personal devotion and in winning others to the Way. Often He would take special pains to impress upon His followers the meaning of some passage in the Bible, and He never ceased to use the Scriptures in His conversation with them. Altogether there are at least sixty-six references to the Old Testament in His dialogues with the disciples in the four Gospels, to say nothing of the more than ninety allusions to it in His speaking with others.[1]

All this served to show the disciples how they too should know and use the Scriptures in their own life. The principles of Bible exhortation were practiced before them so repeatedly that they could not help but catch on to at least some of the rules for basic Scriptural interpretation and application. Moreover, the ability of Jesus to recall so freely Old Testament passages must have impressed the disciples with the necessity of learning the Scriptures by heart, and letting them become the authority for their pronouncements.

In everything it was made abundantly clear that the Word written in the Scriptures and the Word spoken by

---

1. These are separate instances of His spoken Word in which some reference is made to the Old Testament, either by direct quotation, allusion to some event, or language similar to words used in Jewish Scriptures. Counting duplications in parallel accounts of the same event there are altogether about 160 references in the Four Gospels where Jesus alludes to the Bible of His day. Furthermore, two-thirds of the Old Testament books are included in these references. In view of this, one can conclude that the Word of Christ was thoroughly imbued with the teaching of the old patriarchs, kings, and prophets. His whole thought was cast in the spirit of the inspired writings of His day. See Herman Harrell Horne, *Jesus the Master Teacher* (New York: Association Press, 1920), pp. 93–106; and J. M. Price, *op. cit.*, 8–11, 62–64. Virtually a complete list of these various Old Testament references in the Gospels may be found in A. T. Robertson, *Harmony of the Gospels for Students of the Life of Christ* (New York: Harper, 1922), pp. 295–301.

Christ were not in contradiction, but rather complemented each other. That which Jesus believed was also to be cherished by His disciples. Hence, the Scriptures, coupled with His own utterance, became for them the objective basis of their faith in Christ. Furthermore, it was made clear to them that if they were to continue in His fellowship by the Spirit after He was gone from them in the flesh, they would have to abide in His Word (John 15:7).

SUPREMELY SOUL WINNING

Through this manner of personal demonstration, every aspect of Jesus' personal discipline of life was bequeathed to His disciples,[1] but what perhaps was most important in view of His ultimate purpose was that all the while He was teaching them how to win souls.

Practically everything that Jesus said and did had some relevance to their work of evangelism, either by explaining a spiritual truth or revealing to them how they should deal with men. He did not have to work up teaching situations, but merely took advantage of those about Him, and thus His teaching seemed perfectly realistic. In fact, for the most part, the disciples were absorbing it without even knowing that they were being trained to win people under like conditions for God.

---

1. The limits of this discussion do not permit an exhaustive treatment of all the practices of Jesus which affected His life. His manner in regard to teaching the disciples to pray and use the Bible is mentioned only as an example of how careful He was to prepare His followers for service. To adequately cover the subject, one must consider His practice of worship, His concern for the rituals and laws of society, His attitude in regard to civil and social responsibilities, just to mention a few. But the point is that in all these things Jesus taught His disciples how to live a relevant and victorious life in the midst of a pagan world.

TEACHING NATURALLY

This point, already alluded to several times, cannot be emphasized too much. Jesus was so much the Master in His teaching that He did not let His method obscure His lesson. He let His truth call attention to itself, and not the presentation.[1] His method in this respect was to conceal the fact that He even had a method. He was His method.

This may be hard to imagine in this day of professional techniques and sure-fire gimmicks. In some quarters, it would almost appear we would be unable to proceed without a well-illustrated handbook or multicolored chart showing us what to do. The least we might expect is a class in soul winning. Yet, strange as it may seem, the disciples never had any of these things now considered so essential for the work.

All the disciples had to teach them was a Teacher Who practiced with them what He expected them to learn. Evangelism was lived before them in spirit and in technique. Watching Him, they learned what it was all about. He led them to recognize the need inherent in all classes of people, and the best methods of approaching them.

---

1. Numerous authors have sought to analyze the teaching techniques of Jesus, and the student who wants to pursue this subject further would do well to consult some of these works, such as, D. M. Ross, *The Teaching of Jesus* (Edinburgh: T. & T. Clark, 1904), esp. pp. 46–59; George Barker Stevens, *The Teaching of Jesus* (New York: Macmillan, 1918), pp. 33–46; Charles Francis McKay, *The Art of Jesus as a Teacher* (Philadelphia: The Judson Press, 1930); and Luther Allan Weigle, *Jesus and the Educational Method* (New York: Abingdon, 1939). Works by Horne, Squires, Richardson, and Price, mentioned in an earlier footnote, also provide very helpful insights.

They observed how He drew people to Himself; how He won their confidence and inspired their faith; how He opened to them the way of salvation and called them to a decision. In all types of situations and among all kinds of people, rich and poor, healthy and sick, friend and foe alike, the disciples watched the Master Soul-winner at work. It wasn't outlined on the blackboard of a stuffy classroom nor written up in a "Do It Yourself" manual. His method was so real and practical that it just came naturally.

CLASSES ALWAYS IN SESSION

This was as true in His approach to the masses as His way of dealing with individuals. The disciples were always there to observe His Word and deed. If the particular approach was not clear, all they had to do was to ask the Master to explain it to them. For example, after Jesus told the story of the sower to "a very great multitude" (Mark 4:1f.; cf., Matt. 13:1–9; Luke 8:4–8), His disciples "asked Him what this parable might be" (Luke 8:9; cf., Mark 4:10; Matt. 13:10). Whereupon Jesus proceeded to explain to them in detail the meaning of the analogies used in the illustration. In fact, judging from the printed Text, He spent three times the amount of time explaining this story to the disciples than He did in giving the initial lesson to the crowd (Matt. 13:10–23; Mark 4:10–25; Luke 8:9–18).[1]

---

1. Other instances of this same thing follow the parable of the tares (Matt. 13:36f.); His rebuke to the Pharisees for making void the Word of God by their traditions (Matt. 15:15f.); the lesson on the rich young fool (Luke 12:22f.); the parable of the rich man and Lazarus (Luke 17:1f.); His Word to the Pharisees concerning the coming of the Kingdom (Luke 17:22f.); and the matter of divorce according to the law of Moses (Mark 10:10f; Matt. 19:7f).

When the disciples seemed reluctant to confess their bewilderment, then Jesus often would have to take the initiative in clearing up the problem. The story of the rich young ruler is a typical incident. After Jesus dealt with him rather sternly, and the young ruler went away sorrowful because he loved his riches more than the Kingdom of God, Jesus turned to His disciples and said: "It is hard for a rich man to enter into the kingdom of heaven" (Matt. 19:23; cf., Mark 10:23; Luke 18:24). "The disciples were amazed at His Words" (Mark 10:24). This led to an extended conversation in which Jesus explained the reason for His approach to this good moral man, while also using the opportunity to apply the principle to their own profession of faith (Mark 10:24–31; Matt. 19:24–20:16; Luke 18:25–30).

THE PRINCIPLE IN FOCUS

The method of Jesus here was more than a continuous sermon; it was an object lesson as well. This was the secret of His influence in teaching. He did not ask anyone to do or be anything which first He had not demonstrated in His own life, thereby not only proving its workability, but also its relevance to His mission in life. And this He was able to do because He was constantly with His disciples. His training classes were never dismissed. Everything which He said and did was a personal lesson in reality, and since the disciples were there to notice it, they were learning practically every moment of their waking day.

How else will His Way ever be learned? It is well enough to tell people what we mean, but it is infinitely better to show them how to do it. People are looking for a demonstration, not an explanation.

THE PRINCIPLE APPLIED TODAY

When it is all boiled down, those of us who are seeking to train men must be prepared to have them follow us, even as we follow Christ (I Cor. 11:1). We are the exhibit (Phil. 3:17f.; I Thess. 2:7, 8; II Tim. 1:13). They will do those things which they hear and see in us (Phil. 4:9). Given time, it is possible through this kind of leadership to impart our way of living to those who are constantly with us.

We must take this truth to our lives. There can be no shirking or evading of our personal responsibility to show the way to those we are training, and this revelation must include the practical outworking in life of the deeper realities of the Spirit. This is the Master's method, and nothing else will ever suffice to train others to do His work.

Yet, as we know, mere knowledge is not enough. There comes a time for action. To disregard this privilege can nullify all that has been acquired in the process of learning. Indeed, knowledge unapplied to living can become a stumbling-stone to further truth. No one better understood this than the Master. He was training men to do a job, and when they knew enough to get started, He saw to it that they did something about it. The application of this principle is so pronounced that it needs to be considered as another part of His strategy of conquest through trained and spiritually alert men.

6 · Delegation

HE ASSIGNED THEM WORK

Jesus was always building up in His ministry to the time when His disciples would have to take over His work, and go out into the world with the redeeming Gospel. This plan was progressively made clear as they followed Him.

The patience with which Jesus brought this out to His disciples reflects upon His consideration for their ability to learn. He was never premature in His insistence upon action. The first invitation to the disciples to follow Him said nothing about going out and evangelizing the world, although this was His plan from the beginning. His method was to get the disciples into a vital experience with God, and to show them how He worked, before telling them they had to do it.

On the other hand, Jesus did not discourage their spontaneous reactions to bear witness to their faith, and in fact, He seemed delighted that they wanted to bring others to know what they had found. Andrew got Peter, Philip found Nathaniel, Matthew invited his friends to a feast in his house—and Jesus responded to these new introductions with gladness. It is well, also, to note that on several occasions Jesus specifically asked those who were helped by His ministry to say something about it to others. However, in none of these early instances is the real purpose of their life of witnessing made a matter of explicit command.

He used His disciples in other ways to help along His work, such as caring for the manual burdens of getting food and arranging accommodations for the group as they followed Him. He also let them baptize some people who were aroused by His message (John 4:2).[1] Outside of this, however, it is rather startling to observe in the Gospels that these early disciples really did not do much more than watch Jesus work for a year or more. He kept the vision before them by His activity, and in His call again to the four fishermen He reminded them that following Him they were to be fishers of men (Mark 1:17; Matt. 4:19; Luke 5:10), but it does not seem that they did much about it. For that matter, even after they were formally ordained to the ministry a few months later (Mark 3:14–19; Luke 6:13–16), they still showed no evidence of doing any evangelistic work on their own. This observation perhaps should cause us to be more patient with new converts who follow us.

---

1. I cannot restrain the observation here that the disciples of Jesus were given the privilege of administering the rite of baptism considerably before they were ordained to preach. If we were to deduce from this a rule of ecclesiastical policy, it would imply certainly that the preaching ministry is more significant and wrought with more dangers and privileges than a ministry of the sacraments, at least, of baptism. Anyone thus entrusted with the sacred ministry of the Word has a much more responsible position than merely administering baptism, and thus the greater responsibility should include the lesser. The application of this policy, however, would have some far-reaching ramifications in many communions of the modern Church.

FIRST EVANGELISTIC MISSION OF THE TWELVE

But as Jesus was beginning His third general tour of Galilee (Mark 6:6; Matt. 9:35), He doubtless realized that the time had come when His disciples could join Him more directly in the work. They had seen enough at least to get started. They needed now to put into practice what they had seen their Master do. So "He called unto Him the twelve, and began to send them forth" (Mark 6:7; cf., Matt. 10:5; Luke 9:1, 2). Like a mother eagle teaching her young to fly by pushing them out of the nest, Jesus pushed His disciples out into the world to try their own wings.

BRIEFING INSTRUCTIONS

Before letting them go, however, Jesus gave them some briefing instructions on their mission. What He said to them on this occasion is very important to this study because, in a sense, He outlined for them explicitly what He had been teaching implicitly all the time.

He first reaffirmed His purpose for their lives. They were to go and "preach the Kingdom of God, and to heal the sick" (Luke 9:1, 2; cf., Matt. 10:1; Mark 6:7). Nothing was new in this commission, but it did serve to further clarify their task. However, their new instructions did emphasize more the immediacy of their task with the announcement that the "Kingdom was at hand" (Matt. 10:7). It also spelled out more completely the scope of their authority by telling them not only to heal, but to "cleanse the lepers, cast out devils, and raise the dead" (Matt. 10:8).

But Jesus did not leave it at this. He went on to tell

them who to see first. "Go not into any way of the Gentiles, and enter not into any city of the Samaritans; but
go rather to the lost sheep of the house of Israel" (Matt.
10:5, 6). It was as though Jesus was telling His disciples to
go where they would find the most susceptible audience
to hear their message. This is the way that Jesus proceeded in His ministry, although as time went on He
did not bind Himself by it. Since kinsmen were those
most like them in cultural and religious background, it is
only natural that they start with them. Interestingly
enough, a few months later, when the seventy are sent
out, this parting injunction was not repeated, perhaps
indicating it was time then to go beyond these natural ties
in pressing the claims of Christ.

As to their support, they were to trust God to supply
their needs. They were told to render their services freely,
remembering how they had also freely received from
their Lord (Matt. 10:8). Consequently, Jesus instructed
them not to burden themselves unnecessarily with a lot of
excess baggage and provisions (Matt. 10:9, 10; Mark 6:8,
9; Luke 9:3). As they were faithful to God, He would
see to it that they were supplied their needs. "The laborer
is worthy of his food" (Matt. 10:10).

FOLLOW HIS METHOD

The plan of Jesus is even more specific to His disciples
in His instructions to find some friendly person in each
town they visited, and there live as long as they continued
their evangelistic work in the area. "Into whatsoever city
or village ye shall enter, search out who in it is worthy;
and there abide till ye go forth" (Matt. 10:11; cf., Mark
6:10; Luke 9:4). In effect, the disciples were told to concentrate their time upon the most promising individuals

in each town who would thereby be able to follow up
their work after they had gone. This was to receive
priority over everything else. In fact, if they could not
find someone who would take them in, they were specifically instructed to shake off the dust on their feet as
a testimony against them. It would be "more tolerable
for the land of Sodom and Gomorrah in the day of judgment, than for that city" (Matt. 10:14, 15; cf., Luke 9:5;
Mark 6:11). This principle of establishing a beachhead in
a new place of labor by getting with a potentially key
follow-up leader is not to be minimized. Jesus had lived
by it with His own disciples, and He expected them to
do the same. His whole plan of evangelism depended
upon it, and those places which refused the disciples opportunity to practice this principle actually brought the
judgment of utter darkness upon themselves.

EXPECT HARDSHIP

The fact that some men would refuse the disciples'
ministry only accentuated Jesus' warning of the treatment they could expect to receive. "Beware of men: for
they will scourge you; yea and before governors and
kings shall ye be brought for my sake, for a testimony to
them and to the Gentiles" (Matt. 10:17, 18). This was
only natural, since "a disciple is not above his Master, or
a servant above his Lord" (Matt. 10:24). The rulers had
called Jesus Beelzebub, and those of His household could
not expect any less abuse (Matt. 10:25). This was to say
again that His way was contrary to the accepted pattern
of worldly wisdom. Therefore they would be hated of
all men (Matt. 10:22, 23). Nevertheless, Jesus told them
to "fear not." God would never desert them. And though
their witness was wrought with grave danger to their

lives, the Holy Spirit would enable them to meet emergencies (Matt. 10:20, 21). No matter what happened to them, Jesus assured them that everyone who confessed Him before men would be remembered before His Father in heaven (Matt. 10:32).

One cannot help being impressed with the realistic way that Jesus never let His disciples underestimate the strength of the enemy, nor the natural resistance of men to His redeeming Gospel. They were not looking for trouble. Indeed, His admonition to them to be "as wise as serpents, and harmless as doves" (Matt. 10:16) underscored the need for propriety and tactfulness, but in spite of all their precautions, the fact remained that the world was not likely to receive the disciples with favor when they faithfully preached the Gospel. They were sent "as sheep in the midst of wolves" (Matt. 10:16).

A DIVIDING GOSPEL

It is significant, too, that Jesus reminded them of the decisive nature of the Gospel invitation. There could be no compromise with sin, and for this reason, anyone holding out on God was sure to be disturbed by their preaching. They were not hand-shaking emissaries maintaining the status quo of complacency. Rather Jesus said: "Think not that I came to send peace on the earth: I came not to send peace, but a sword. For I came to set a man at variance against his father, and the daughter against her mother, and the daughter-in-law against her mother-in-law; and a man's foes shall be they of his own household. He that loveth father or mother more than Me is not worthy of Me: and he that loveth son or daughter more than Me is not worthy of Me. And he that doth not take his cross and follow after Me, is not worthy of

Me" (Matt. 10:34–38). If the disciples had any notions prior to this time about the easy nature of their work, it was certainly dispelled now. They were going forth with a revolutionary Gospel, and when it was obeyed, it effected a revolutionary change in people and their society.

ONE WITH CHRIST

The point Jesus made in all these instructions was that the mission of His disciples was not different in principle or method from His own. He began by giving them His own authority and power to do His work (Mark 6:7; Matt. 10:1; Luke 9:1), and He closed by assuring them that what they were doing was as though He was doing it Himself. "He that receiveth you receiveth Me, and he that receiveth Me receiveth Him that sent Me" (Matt. 10:40; cf., John 13:20). Think of this identity! The disciples were to be the actual representatives of Christ as they went forth. So clear was this association that if someone even gave a child a cup of cold water in the name of a disciple, that act of mercy would be rewarded (Matt. 10:42).

TWO BY TWO

These were the instructions that Jesus gave to His disciples. But before they went out, He teamed them up in pairs of two (Mark 6:7).[1] Doubtless this plan was in-

1. The plan of going out in pairs seemed to be a practice followed often in the Gospels. For example, two disciples were sent to find the colt for Jesus to use in entering Jerusalem (Luke 19:29). Peter and John together are sent to make ready the Passover (Luke 22:8). It is probable that James and John were together on their mission before Jesus into Samaria since they are the ones loud in indignation at their reception (Luke 9:52, 54). James I. Vance in his little volume, *The College of Apostles* (New York: Fleming

tended to provide for His disciples needed companionship along the way. Together they could help one another, and when adverse circumstances greeted them as surely often would be the case, they could still find solace among themselves. It reflects again the characteristic concern of Jesus for togetherness.

"And they departed, and went throughout the villages, preaching the Gospel, and healing everywhere" (Luke 9:6; cf., Mark 6:12). The little group of disciples were finally started in the active ministry of Christ on their own.

Of course, this was no excuse for Jesus to neglect His own work. He never asked anyone to do something which He was unwilling to do. So as the disciples went out, the Master likewise "departed thence to teach and preach in their cities" (Matt. 11:1).

THE MISSION OF SEVENTY

Not many months after this "seventy others" were sent out again two by two to witness for their Lord (Luke

---

H. Revell, 1896), even attempts to view all the apostles in terms of pairs, making altogether six groups of two within the company. His idea is that the disciples were matched up in order to complement the other's virtues and to minimize the other's faults. His grouping put together Peter the extremist with Andrew the conservative; James the elder with John the youth; Philip the dullard with Bartholomew the sage; Thomas the man of doubts with Matthew the man of strong conviction; James the champion of duty with Jude the champion of doctrine; and Simon the Zealot with Judas the traitor. The support for this supposition rests largely on the listing of the apostles in pairs by Matthew (Matt. 10:2–4). Latham, *op. cit.*, p. 162. In all fairness, I think that we must recognize that this grouping is mostly hypothetical. Nevertheless, it is a matter of record that the Book of Acts represents the apostles and missionaries of the Church traveling in groups of two or more.

10:1). It is not known for sure just who these other disciples were, but the indications are that they included the original twelve. The size of the group also indicates that this was due in measure to the increased activity of the twelve in witnessing for Christ.

Again the instructions given to this larger group were essentially the same as those delivered earlier to the twelve (Luke 10:2–16). One addition in this new commission was the reminder that they were going "into every city and place, whither He Himself was about to come" (Luke 10:1). That is, the disciples were forerunners for their Lord, setting things up for His ministry. This detail had been impressed upon them a few weeks before while they were on a trip to Samaria (Luke 9:52), so actually it was not something with which they had no previous knowledge. It merely indicated again that they all were to practice what they had learned to be their Master's strategy of evangelism.

POST-RESURRECTION COMMANDS

The principle of giving evangelistic work assignments to His disciples was conclusively demonstrated just before He returned to Heaven after His crucifixion and resurrection. On at least four occasions as He met with His disciples He told them to go out and do His work. It was first mentioned to the disciples, with the exception of Thomas, on that first Easter evening as they were assembled in the Upper Room. After Jesus had showed the astonished disciples His nail-scarred hands and feet (Luke 24:38–40), and had partaken of the meal with them (Luke 24:41–43), He then said: "Peace be unto you: as the Father hath sent Me, even so send I you" (John 20:21), whereupon Jesus assured them again of the promise and authority of the Holy Spirit to do the work.

A little later as Jesus had breakfast with His disciples by the Sea of Tiberias, He told Peter three times to feed His sheep (John 21:15, 16, 17). This admonition was interpreted to the big fisherman as the proof of his love to the Master.

On a mountain in Galilee He gave His great commission to, not only the eleven disciples (Matt. 28:16), but also to the whole church numbering then about 500 brethren (I Cor. 15:6). It was a clear proclamation of His strategy of world conquest. "All authority hath been given unto Me in heaven and in earth. Go ye therefore, and make disciples of all the nations, baptizing them into the Name of the Father and of the Son and of the Holy Ghost, teaching them to observe all things whatsoever I commanded you: and lo, I am with you always, even unto the end of the world" (Matt. 28:18–20; cf., Mark 16: 15–18).

Finally, before He ascended back to the Father, Jesus went over the whole thing again with His disciples for the last time, showing them how things had to be fulfilled while He was with them (Luke 24:44, 45). His suffering and death, as well as His resurrection from the dead the third day, was all according to schedule (Luke 24:46). Jesus went on to show His disciples "that repentance and remission of sin should be preached in His Name unto all nations, beginning from Jerusalem" (Luke 24:47). And for the fulfillment of this divine purpose, the disciples were no less a part than their Master. They were to be the human instruments announcing the good tidings, and the Holy Spirit was to be God's personal empowerment for their mission. "Ye shall receive power when the Holy Ghost is come upon you: and ye shall be my witness both in Jerusalem, and in all Judea and Samaria, and unto the uttermost part of the earth" (Acts 1:8; cf., Luke 24:48, 49).

THE PRINCIPLE IS CLEAR

Clearly Jesus did not leave the work of evangelism subject to human impression or convenience. To His disciples it was a definite command, perceived by impulse at the beginning of their discipleship, but progressively clarified in their thinking as they followed Him, and finally spelled out in no uncertain terms. No one who followed Jesus very far could escape this conclusion. It was so then; it is so today.

Christian disciples are sent men—sent out in the same work of world evangelism to which the Lord was sent, and for which He gave His life. Evangelism is not an optional accessory to our life. It is the heartbeat of all that we are called to be and do. It is the commission of the church which gives meaning to all else that is undertaken in the Name of Christ. With this purpose clearly in focus, everything which is done and said has glorious fulfillment of God's redemptive purpose—educational institutions, social programs, hospitals, church meetings of any kind—everything done in the Name of Christ has its justification in fulfilling this mission.

THE PRINCIPLE APPLIED TODAY

But it is not enough to make this an ideal. It must be given tangible expression by those who are following the Savior. The best way to be sure that this is done is to give practical work assignments and expect them to be carried out. This gets men started, and where they already have seen their work demonstrated in the life of their teacher, there is no reason why the assignment cannot be completed. When the church takes this lesson to heart, and gets down to business with evangelism, then those in the pews will soon start moving out for God.

However, the fact that one starts the work is no assurance that he will keep it up. Once inertia is overcome, it is still necessary to keep one moving, and going in the right direction. Certainly the assignments that Jesus gave His disciples, at least at first, were no discharge from His school of training. They had much more to learn before they could be considered ready for graduation, and until that time came, He had no intention of turning them loose from His personal direction. His concern at this point was so explicit and His method of dealing with it so pronounced that it needs to be considered as another step in His strategy of ultimate victory.

7 · Supervision

HE KEPT CHECK ON THEM

Jesus made it a point to get with His disciples follow-ing their tours of service to hear their reports and to share with them the blessedness of His ministry in doing the same thing. In this sense, one might say that His teaching rotated between instruction and assignment. What time He was with them, He was helping them to understand the reason for some previous action or getting them ready for some new experience. His questions, illustrations, warnings, and admonitions were calculated to bring out those things that they needed to know in order to fulfill His work, which was the evangelization of the world.

Accordingly, not long after the twelve were sent out, they gathered themselves "together with Jesus" to tell "what things they had done" (Mark 6:30; Luke 9:10). It would appear from the Bible that this reunion was pre-arranged, and hence, the initial solo excursion of the dis-ciples was merely a field assignment as they continued their training with the Master.

The regrouping of the disciples following their evange-listic tour, of course, provided them some needed rest in body and soul. As to how long the disciples had been out, the Scripture does not say. Perhaps a few days, even a week. The time element here is not the important thing. What does matter though, as the Record shows, is that after the disciples were sent out to work, they were expected to share their experiences, later, with the group.

Similarly, after the seventy went out, Jesus called them back to report on their work during the visitation. "And the seventy returned with joy, saying, Lord, even the devils are subject unto us in Thy Name" (Luke 10:17). On the previous mission of the twelve, no mention is made of any spectacular success in their work, but on this occasion they had a rousing report of triumph. Perhaps the difference was the additional experience which the disciples had gained.

Nothing could have given Jesus more joy than this. Visualizing the victory ultimately assured by their work, Jesus said: "I beheld Satan falling as lightning from heaven" (Luke 10:18). "In that same hour He rejoiced in the Holy Spirit" and then lifted up His voice in praise to God for what had been done (Luke 10:21, 22). This was what Jesus had been working for all these long months, and now He was beginning to see His labors show fruit. Yet, to show how Jesus was alert to make experiences teach truth, even this occasion was used to caution the disciples against pride in their accomplishments. As he put it, "Howbeit in this rejoice not, that the spirits are subject unto you; but rejoice that your names are written in heaven" (Luke 10:20).

CONTINUOUS REVIEW AND APPLICATION

What is seen here so vividly in these checkup sessions following the disciples' visitation merely brings into bold relief a strategy of Jesus throughout His ministry. As He reviewed some experience which the disciples had He would bring out some practical application of it to their lives.

Take, as an illustration, the way He responded to the futile efforts of some of His disciples to heal an afflicted boy. This incident was precipitated while Jesus was on the Mount of Transfiguration, with Peter, James, and John. In His absence, the other disciples had tried to heal a demon-possessed boy brought to them by the father. The case was too much for their faith, and when Jesus returned to see how things were getting along, He found the distraught father with the sick child having a fit before the helpless disciples. Jesus, of course, took care of the boy, but He did not let the occasion pass without giving the frustrated disciples a much needed lesson on how they, through more prayer and fasting, should have laid hold upon God's faithfulness (Mark 9:17–29; Matt. 17:14–20; Luke 9:37–43).

Or, again, think of the way He recalled their part in feeding the multitude to impress upon them His power to do all things, while also teaching them a vital lesson concerning spiritual discernment (Mark 6:30–44; 7:31–8:9, 13–21; Matt. 14:13–21; 15:29–38; Luke 9:10–17; John 6:1–13). It came about as they were going across the sea of Galilee in a boat immediately following the Master's severe denunciation of the chronic sign-seeking attitude of the religious sects of His day (Mark 8:10–12; Matt. 15:39–16:4). Jesus, doubtless feeling a great heaviness because of the incident on the other side of the lake, turned to His disciples and said: "Take heed, beware of the leaven of the Pharisees." But the spiritually dull disciples, growing hungry for food, and having only one loaf of bread with them, thought that they should not buy bread from these unbelieving people, and therefore wondered where their next meal was coming from. Realizing that they had missed completely the spiritual lesson of His remarks intended to warn them against unbelief, Jesus said: "O ye of little faith, why reason ye among yourselves because ye have no bread? Do ye not yet perceive, neither understand? Have ye your heart hardened? Having eyes, see ye not? And having ears, hear ye not? And do ye not remember? When I broke the five loaves among the five thousand, how many baskets ful of broken pieces took ye up?" The disciples answered, "Twelve" (Mark 8:19).

Doubtless this brought clearly to mind that day when the disciples seated the multitudes for dinner, and then saw Jesus perform the miracle of the loaves.[1] They remembered, too, how He employed them to distribute the provisions so that everybody had enough, and then to gather up what was left. Indeed, it was a vivid recollection, for each one of the twelve had a basket full of food when it was all over. Similarly, they remembered how that they had seven baskets left over from feeding the four thousand. With this evidence of Jesus' miraculous power there could be no doubt about His ability to feed them with their loaf of bread if it was necessary. "Then they understood how that He bade them, not beware of

---

1. Before Jesus fed the five thousand, He first asked the disciples to give the people something to eat. This was done purposely to show them their little faith (John 6:6), and also to impress upon them the problem created thereby. It was only after the disciples were convinced of their utter helplessness in the face of this situation that Jesus intervened, yet even then He used the disciples in His solution to the problem.

the leaven of bread, but of the teaching of the Pharisees and Sadducees" (Matt. 16:12).

LESSONS ON PATIENCE

One of the most penetrating of the Lord's correctional lectures following the disciples' activity was in connection with their attitude toward others in the work who were not members of the apostolic company. It seems that in the course of their travels they had run across some people casting out demons in Jesus' Name, but since these persons were not of their denomination, the disciples had severely rebuked them for it (Mark 9:38; Luke 9:49). Doubtless Jesus' disciples felt they were doing the right thing, but when it was reported to the Master, He felt constrained to give them an extended discourse on the dangers of discouraging any sincere work on His behalf (Mark 9:39–50; Matt. 18:6–14). "Forbid them not," Jesus said, "for He that is not against you is with you" (Luke 9:50). Then making His point apply more generally to all innocent people, especially children, He went on to say, "Whosoever shall cause one of these little ones that believe on me to stumble, it were better for him if a great millstone were hanged about his neck and he were cast into the sea" (Mark 9:42). "It is not the will of your Father which is in heaven, that one of these little ones should perish" (Matt. 18:14).

On another excursion, the disciples encountered some resistance to their work while on an assignment for their Lord in Samaria. Reacting impulsively to destroy the people, they wanted to call down fire from heaven (Luke 9:51–54). But Jesus, who was standing nearby, "turned and rebuked them," adding, "Ye know not what manner of Spirit ye are of. For the Son of Man came not to de-

stroy men's lives, but to save them" (Luke 9:55, 56).
And then showing His disciples how they might solve this
kind of problem, "they went to another village" (Luke
9:56).

THE PRINCIPLE OBSERVED

Many other illustrations could be cited to show how
Jesus checked up on the actions and reactions of His disciples as they faced various difficult situations. He kept after
them constantly, giving them increasingly more attention
as His ministry on earth came to a close. He would not
let them rest in success or in failure. No matter what they
did, there was always more to do and to learn. He rejoiced
in their success, but nothing less than world conquest was
His goal, and to that end He always superintended their
efforts.[1]

Here was on-the-job training at its best. Jesus would let
His followers have some experience or make some observation of their own, and then He would use this as a start-
ing point to teach a lesson of discipleship. The fact that
they tried to do His work, even though they may have
failed at it, gave them greater awareness of their deficien-
cies, and hence they were more disposed to the Master's
correction. Moreover, their encounter with life situations
enabled Jesus to pinpoint His teaching upon specific needs
and to spell it out in the concrete terms of practical experience. One always appreciates an education more after
he has had the opportunity to apply what he knows.

The important thing about all this supervisionary work

---

1. It is significant that He was careful to teach them that the Holy
Spirit would continue to supervise their work after He had turned
them loose from His incarnate direction. The Christian worker
never is without personal supervision.

of Jesus was that He kept the disciples going on toward the goal He had set for them. He did not expect more from His disciples than they could do, but He did expect their best, and this He expected always to be improved as they grew in knowledge and grace. His plan of teaching, by example, assignment, and constant checkup, was calculated to bring out the best that was in them.

THE PRINCIPLE APPLIED TODAY

No less patient yet determined supervision is needed today among those who are seeking to train others for evangelism. One dare not assume that the work will be done merely because he has shown a willing worker how to do it, and then sent him out with a glowing expectation of results. Innumerable things could happen to frustrate and sidetrack the work, and unless these matters are dealt with realistically by competent and understanding people, the worker may easily become discouraged and defeated. Likewise, many experiences of grace which bring delight to the soul need to be clarified and deepened as their meaning is interpreted in the light of the total world mission of Christ. It is thus crucial that those engaging in the work of evangelism have personal supervision and guidance until such time as they are matured enough to carry on alone.

KEEP THE VISION CLEAR

We must always remember, too, that the goal is world conquest. We dare not let a lesser concern capture our strategy of the moment. All too many times one has been brought to the place of service only to be discharged with no further training or inspiration. The result is that his activity becomes localized in a feverish round of excitement. There is no growth. The potential ability resident in the worker is not developed, and before long a promising leader is spoiled for want of supervision. Success is lost on the eve of victory. What once looked so good eventually becomes a stumbling stone to the best.

Undoubtedly much of our effort for the Kingdom is dissipated for this reason. We fail, not because we do not try to do something, but because we let our little efforts become an excuse for not doing more. The result is that we lose by default the advantage of years of hard work and sacrifice.

When will we learn the lesson of Christ not to be satisfied merely with the firstfruits of those who are sent out to witness? Disciples must be brought to maturity. There can be no substitute for total victory, and our field is the world. We have not been called to hold the fort, but to storm the heights. It is in this light that the final step in Jesus' strategy of evangelism can be understood.

8 · Reproduction

HE EXPECTED THEM TO REPRODUCE

Jesus intended for the disciples to produce His likeness in and through the Church being gathered out of the world. Thus His ministry in the Spirit would be duplicated manyfold by His ministry in the lives of His disciples. Through them and others like them it would continue to expand in an ever enlarging circumference until the multitudes might know in some similar way the opportunity which they had known with the Master. By this strategy the conquest of the world was only a matter of time and their faithfulness to His plan.

Jesus had built into His disciples the structure of a church that would challenge and triumph over all the powers of death and Hell. It had started small like a grain of mustard seed, but it would grow in size and strength until it became a tree "greater than all the herbs" (Matt. 13:32; cf., Mark 4:32; Luke 13:18, 19). Jesus did not expect that everyone would be saved (He recognized realistically the rebellion of men in spite of grace), but He did foresee the day when the Gospel of salvation in His Name would be proclaimed convincingly to every creature. Through that testimony His Church militant would someday be the Church universal even as it would become the Church triumphant.

It was not going to be an easy conquest. Many would suffer persecution and martyrdom in the battle. Yet no matter how great the trials through which His people would pass, and how many temporal skirmishes were lost in the struggle, the ultimate victory was certain. His Church would win in the end.[1] Nothing could permanently prevail against it "or be strong to its detriment, or hold out against it" (Matt. 16:18, *Amplified New Testament*).

VICTORY THROUGH WITNESSING

This incredible confidence in the future was based upon His knowledge of those who worshipped Him in the present. He knew that His disciples had learned at least the essence of His glory. Peter, the spokesman for the band, had summed it up in his affirmation to Jesus: "Thou art the Christ, the Son of the living God" (Matt. 16:16; cf., Mark 8:29; Luke 9:20). Here was a truth indestructible, and it was upon this foundation that Jesus envisioned how His victory would be won, as He replied: "Thou art Peter, and upon this rock I will build my church" (Matt. 16:18).

The force of these words indicates the significance of human initiative in bringing it to pass. Irrespective of the

---

1. Lest someone misconstrue this optimism to suppose that the evangelization of the world stressed here negates the need or the fact of Christ's glorious second coming, let me reiterate that the preaching of the Gospel only prepares the way for the Lord's return (Matt. 24:14). It neither discounts the personal intervention of Christ at the end time nor implies that the Kingdom will come as a result of human ingenuity. This is true regardless of what particular millennial view one might hold.

excitement aroused by the ecclesiastical overtones of the
passage, we should agree, at least, that Jesus' words were
addressed to a person who personally had made an affirmation of faith in his Lord.[1] Indeed, this realization of his

---

1. The personal nature of the address is sometimes obscured by
those who seek to avoid any suggestion that Peter was given su-
premacy in the Church. Such concern is unnecessary for there is
nothing in the passage, or anywhere else in the Bible, that lends
credence to the Roman Catholic pretensions for the Papacy. To
say even that the "rock" refers to Peter, as many exegetes do,
merely underscopes his prominence and leadership in affirming the
faith of Christ. See this view in A. B. Bruce, *The Expositor's Greek
Testament*, ed. by Nicoll, Reprint (Grand Rapids, Eerdmans), pp.
224, 225; Philip Vollmer, *The Modern Life of Christ* (New York,
Revell, 1912), pp. 162, 163; also the commentaries of Meyer, Al-
ford, Brown, and Bengel. However, other scholars prefer to dis-
associate from Peter the "rock" upon which the Church is here
said to be built. They follow several lines of interpretation, especially the idea that the "rock" means Peter's confession of faith.
An example is A. T. Robertson, *Word Pictures in the New Testament*, I (New York, Harper, 1930), pp. 131–133; also the commentaries of Luther and Clark, as well as the *Pilgrim Bible*. Closely
akin to this view, and often intermingled with it, is the opinion
that the "rock" is Christ Himself. For example, the notes in *Berkeley and Scofield* Bibles support this position as also does Augustine
and Jerome. Others believe that it is applied to Peter as a representative of all believers. An example of this interpretation is John
Calvin, *Commentary on a Harmony of the Evangelists*, II, Reprint
(Grand Rapids, Eerdmans, 1949), p. 291. A number of these men
make much of the fact that in the Greek text the word "Peter"
(πέτρος) is in the masculine gender, while the word translated
"rock" (πέτρα) is in the feminine. This distinction makes it possible from the use of the words elsewhere to see Peter as "a piece
of rock formation" in contrast to the "rock formation itself" upon
which the Church was to rest. However, regardless of one's view
at this point, the fact still remains that Peter was spoken to personally by Christ, and he could not have been considered even as
a piece of the rock had he not personally affirmed his faith in
Christ's deity. This conclusion seems to me to stand as an obvious
truth beyond any of the interpretations given to the "rock" cited
above.

Master being the very Son of God was not something which Peter had worked up himself, as Jesus made so clear (Matt. 16:17). Nevertheless, the experience of that revelation in his life was quite definitely located in his "flesh and blood," and through the faithful expression of that fact to others, the Church of Christ was destined to triumph.[1] How could it perish? The apostle's faith in the living Christ was so imbedded in his life that it had solidified into a rock—a rock which Peter recognized to be His Lord, "the Chief Cornerstone," upon which all believers were "living stones" in the construction of His Church (1 Peter 2:4–8; cf., Eph. 2:20–22).[2]

However, we must not fail to see the direct relation between bearing witness of Christ and the ultimate victory over the world. One cannot come without the other. Bringing these two dynamic facts together by the power of the Holy Spirit is the climactic genius of Jesus' strategy of evangelism.

THE PRINCIPLE OBSERVED

It all comes back to His disciples. They were the vanguard of His enveloping movement. "Through their word" He expected others to believe on Him (John

---

1. See Peter Lange for an interesting analysis of the way Peter's faithfulness of confession is regarded as the proper interpretation of the "rock," which amounts really to another point of view on this subject. Peter Lange, *Commentary on the Holy Scriptures,* Matthew, Reprint (Grand Rapids, Zondervan), p. 298. The view stated in my presentation here, however, relates to the whole temper of the passage, and not to any particular word.

2. It is noteworthy that Peter himself makes this analogy. Furthermore, the absence of any claim of personal superiority in his letters indicates convincingly that Peter did not understand his Lord as bestowing any special ecclesiastical or spiritual authority upon him.

17:20), and these in turn to pass the word along to others, until in time the world might know Who He was and what He came to do (John 17:21, 23). His whole evangelistic strategy—indeed, the fulfillment of His very purpose in coming into the world, dying on the cross, and rising from the grave—depended upon the faithfulness of His chosen disciples to this task. It did not matter how small the group was to start with so long as they reproduced and taught their disciples to reproduce. This was the way His Church was to win—through the dedicated lives of those who knew the Savior so well that His Spirit and method constrained them to tell others. As simple as it may seem, this was the way the Gospel would conquer. He had no other plan.

THE TEST OF HIS MINISTRY

Here was the acid test. Would His disciples carry on His work after He had gone? Or what might be even more to the point, could they do as good a job without His bodily supervision as they could with it? This may sound like asking too much, but the fact is that until this point was reached in their Christian nurture, Jesus from a purely human point of view could never be sure that His investment in their lives would pay off for the Kingdom. If they failed to impart His Spirit and method to others who would keep this work going, then His ministry with them all these years would soon come to nought.

No wonder Jesus so indelibly impressed upon His disciples the necessity and inevitability of His life reproducing its kind. An illustration of this was the parable of the vine and the branches (John 15:1–17). Here in one of the most simple yet profound analogies of the Lord,

Christ explained that the purpose of both the vine (Himself) and the branches (believers in Him) was to bear fruit. Hence, any branch that did not yield produce was cut off by the husbandman—it was worthless. What is more, those branches which did produce were pruned by the husbandman that they might yield more fruit (John 15:2). It was clear that the life-sustaining power of the vine was not to be bestowed endlessly upon lifeless branches. Any branch that lived on the vine had to produce to survive for that was its intended nature. Jesus then made the application to His disciples. As surely as they were participants in His life, even so they would bear His fruit (John 15:5, 8), and furthermore, their fruit would remain (John 15:16).[1] A barren Christian is a contradiction. A tree is known by its fruit.

This principle was emphasized time and time again throughout His ministry. It was seen as the inevitable reward of His own sacrifice for the world (John 12:24; cf., 17:19). It was made the distinguishing work of those who did the will of His Father in heaven (Matt. 7:16–23; Luke 6:43–45). It was interpreted as the wages given to His disciples for their work in the harvest (John 4:36–38). It was recognized as that which was denied those who "let the cares of the world, the deceitfulness of riches, and the lusts of other things" choke out the Word of God planted in their hearts (Mark 4:18–20; Matt. 13:22, 23; Luke 8:14, 15). It was observed as the thing lacking in the lives of the Sadducees and Pharisees which made them so

---

1. It is interesting, too, that in this whole passage, every time fruitbearing is mentioned, the word is in the present tense, which means in the Greek text that it is a continuing thing—something that just keeps on reproducing.

wretched in His sight (Matt. 3:7, 8; 12:33, 34; Luke 13: 6–9). In various ways, and among all kinds of people, Jesus called men to evaluate the product of their lives. This was the revelation of what they were. In fact, where fruitbearing is seen in its larger context of reproducing the Christ life in human personality, first in ourselves and then in others, practically everything which the Master said and did pointed to this principle.

THE GREAT COMMISSION

The great commission of Christ given to His Church summed it up in the command to "make disciples of every creature" (Matt. 28:19). The word here indicates that the disciples were to go out into the world and win others who would come to be what they themselves were—disciples of Christ. This mission is emphasized even more when the Greek text of the passage is studied, and it is seen that the words "go," "baptize," and "teach" are all participles which derive their force from the one controlling verb "make disciples."[1] This means that the great commission is not merely to go to the ends of the earth preaching the Gospel (Mark 16:15), nor to baptize a lot of converts into the Name of the Triune God, nor to teach them the precepts of Christ, but to "make disciples"—to build men like themselves who were so constrained by the commission of Christ that they not only followed, but led

---

1. I am indebted to Dr. Roland G. Leavell for first calling this to my attention in his book, *Evangelism, Christ's Imperative Commission* (Nashville: Broadman, 1951), p. 3. The participle "go," however, does stand in a coordinate relationship with the verb which makes it also an imperative. I was surprised to find that none of the commentaries which I checked in reference to this passage seemed to take cognizance of the Greek grammar which justifies the emphasis of the participles cited above.

others to follow His way. Only as disciples were made could the other activities of the commission fulfill their purpose.

PRAY FOR HARVESTERS

Leadership was the emphasis. Jesus had already demonstrated by His own ministry that the deluded masses were ripe for the harvest, but without spiritual shepherds to lead them, how could they ever be won? "Pray ye therefore the Lord of the harvest," Jesus reminded His disciples, "that He will send forth laborers into His harvest" (Matt. 9:37, 38; cf., Luke 10:2). There is almost a note of desperation in these words—a desperation wrung from the sense of the world's desperate need of workers with them who cared for their souls. There is no use to pray for the world. What good would it do? God already loves them and has given His Son to save them. No, there is no use to pray vaguely for the world. The world is lost and blind in sin. The only hope for the world is for men to go to them with the Gospel of Salvation, and having won them to the Savior, not to leave them, but to work with them faithfully, patiently, painstakingly, until they become fruitful Christians savoring the world about them with the Redeemer's love.

THE PRINCIPLE APPLIED TO OUR LIVES

Here finally is where we must all evaluate the contribution that our life and witness is making to the supreme purpose of Him who is the Saviour of the world. Are those who have followed us to Christ now leading others to Him and teaching them to make disciples like ourselves? Note, it is not enough to rescue the perishing, though this is imperative; nor is it sufficient to build up newborn babes in the faith of Christ, although this too is necessary if the first fruit is to endure; in fact, it is not sufficient just to get them out winning souls, as commendable as this work may be. What really counts in the ultimate perpetuation of our work is the faithfulness with which our converts go out and make leaders out of their converts, not simply more followers. Surely we want to win our generation for Christ, and to do it now, but this is not enough. Our work is never finished until it has assured its continuation in the lives of those redeemed by the Evangel.

The test of any work of evangelism thus is not what is seen at the moment, or in the Conference Report, but in the effectiveness with which the work continues in the next generation. Similarly the criteria upon which a Church should measure its success is not how many new names are added to the roll nor how much the budget is increased, but rather how many Christians are actively winning souls and training them to win the multitudes. The ultimate extent of our witness is what matters, and for this reason values can only be measured by eternity.

Is it not time that we all looked again at our lives and ministries from this perspective? As Dawson Trotman would say, "Where are our men?"[1] What are they doing for God? Consider what it would mean to the future of the Church if we had only one true disciple now to show for our labors. Would not this immediately double our influence? And suppose that we made another like ourself, even as the first succeeded in the same way. Would

---

1. Dawson Trotman, *Born to Reproduce* (Lincoln, Nebr.: Back to the Bible Publishers, 1959), p. 42. This little booklet by the founder of the Navigators is something that every person interested in this subject should read.

not this multiply our life four times over? Theoretically, at least, in this manner of multiplication our ministry alone would soon reach multitudes with the Gospel. That is, if that person we had called a disciple truly followed in the steps of the Master.

PROVED BY THE CHURCH

We can be thankful that in those first disciples this was done. They gave the Gospel to the multitudes, but all the while they were building up the fellowship of those who believed. As the Lord added daily to the Church such as were saved, the apostles, like their Master, were developing men to reproduce their ministry to the ends of the earth. The Acts of the Apostles is really just the unfolding in the life of the growing Church the principles of evangelism that have already been outlined here in the life of Christ.

Suffice it to say that the early Church proved that the Master's plan for world conquest worked. So great was the impact of their witness that before the century had passed the pagan society of the day had been shaken to its foundations and growing churches had been established in most centers of population. Had the momentum continued in the evangelistic outreach of the Church that characterized its beginning, within a few centuries the multitudes of the world would have known the touch of the Master's Hand.

SHORTCUTS HAVE FAILED

But times changed, and gradually the simple way of Jesus' evangelism was forced into a new mold. Of course, adaptations of principle are always necessary in the light of changing circumstances, but somehow or other the principles themselves got confused in the desire to give the Evangel a new look. The costly principles of leadership development and reproduction seem to have been submerged beneath the easier strategy of mass recruitment. The nearsighted objective of popular recognition generally took precedence over the long-range goal of reaching the world, and the methods of evangelism employed by the Church collectively and individually have reflected this same momentary outlook. Occasionally, as in times of great spiritual revival, the principles of Jesus' method have come to the fore, but to this observer of church history such periods have been short-lived and have never captured the imagination of the vast majority of churchmen. Jesus' plan has not been disavowed; it has just been ignored. It has been something to remember in venerating the past, but not to be taken seriously as a rule for conduct in the present.

THE ISSUE TODAY

This is our problem of methodology today. Well intended ceremonies, programs, organizations, commissions, and crusades of human ingenuity are trying valiantly to do a job that only can be done by men in the power of the Holy Spirit. This is not to depreciate these noble efforts, for without them the church could not function as she does. Nevertheless, unless the personal mission of the Master is vitally incorporated into the policy and fabric of all these plans, the Church cannot function as she should.

When will we realize that evangelism is not done by something, but by someone. It is an expression of God's love, and God is a Person. His nature, being personal, is only expressed through personality, first revealed fully in Christ, and now expressed through His Spirit in the lives of those yielded to Him. Committees may help to organize and direct it, and to that end they certainly are needed, but the work itself is done by men reaching other men for Christ.

That is why we must say with E. M. Bounds that "men are God's method."[1] Until we have men embued with His Spirit and committed to His plan, none of our methods will work.

This is the new evangelism we need. It is not better methods, but better men—men who know their Redeemer from something more than hearsay—men who see His vision and feel His passion for the world—men who are willing to be nothing in order that He might be everything—men who want only for Christ to produce His life

---

1. E. M. Bounds, *Power Through Prayer,* Reprint (Chicago: Moody Press), p. 7. The account of every great revival and missionary movement in church history will prove the truth of this statement. That is why, outside of the Bible, reading Christian biography will do more to stimulate evangelism than anything else. It would be a good idea to follow a varied and regular plan of reading in this area. Numerous books are available, but among them one should read by all means the *Life and Diary of David Brainerd,* edited by Jonathan Edwards (Chicago: Moody Press, 1949); Dr. and Mrs. Howard Taylor's account of their father in *Hudson Taylor's Spiritual Secret* (London: China Inland Mission, 1950); the *Memoirs of Rev. Charles G. Finney* (New York: Fleming H. Revell Co., 1873), which is still in print; Clarence Wilbur Hall's story of the saintly Brengle, *Portrait of a Prophet* (New York: Salvation Army, 1933); and Jim Elliot's discipline of life compiled from his letters and diary by his wife, Elisabeth Elliot in *Under the Shadow of the Almighty* (New York: Harper & Brothers, 1958). These and other similar true stories of men with vision and dedication will challenge us to do more for God.

in and through them according to His own good pleasure. This finally is the way the Master planned for His objective to be realized on the earth, and where it is carried through by His strategy, the gates of Hell cannot prevail against the evangelization of the world.

EPILOGUE

The Master and Your Plan

LIFE HAS A PLAN

What is the plan of your life? Everyone has to live by some plan. The plan is the organizing principle around which the aim of life is carried out. We may not be conscious of the plan in every action, or even know that we have a plan, but nonetheless our actions invariably unfold some kind of a pattern at the center of things.

When we actually get right down to it, and try to see our objective and how we are going about to achieve it, what we discover may not be very satisfying. But an honest appraisal should cause us all to be more concerned for our calling, at least for the person who believes Jesus' way is the rule by which every action should be tested.

It might well be that some cherished plans of our own making may have to be redirected, or perhaps abandoned altogether. Equally agonizing may be the adjustment of the congregation to the Master's view of the ministry. In all probability our whole concept of success will have to be reevaluated. Nevertheless, if the principles outlined here have any validity at all, they should be understood as guidelines for action. It is only as they are applied to the everyday work of living now that they have any real significance for our lives. To regard them as true means that they must be relevant.

METHODS WILL VARY

Every one of us then should be seeking some way to incorporate the wisdom of Jesus' strategy into our own preferred method of evangelism. Not every one will be led to adopt the same ritual or organization of procedure, nor should we want everyone to fit into the same mold. Variety is in the very structure of the universe, and any method that God is pleased to use is a good method, though this does not exclude the possibility of improvement in our way of doing it. The Master gives us an outline to follow, but He expects us to work out the details according to local circumstances and traditions. This demands every bit of resourcefulness that we have. New and bold approaches will need to be tried as situations change, and not everything tried will work. One unwilling to fail in the determination to find some way to get the job done will never get started, nor will the person afraid to try and try again make much progress.

THE PRIORITY OF MEN

But whatever the particular form our methodology takes, Jesus' life would teach us that finding and training men to reach men must have priority. The multitudes can not know the Gospel unless they have a living witness. Merely giving them an explanation will not suffice. The wandering masses of the world must have a demonstration of what to believe—they must have a man who will stand among them and say, "Follow me, I know the way." Here then is where all our plans must focus. No matter how spiritual our emphasis might otherwise be, the enduring relevance of all that we do will depend upon how well this mission is fulfilled.

Yet we must realize that the kind of manpower that Christ needs does not happen by accident. It requires deliberate planning and concentrated effort. If we are to train men, we must work for them. We must seek them. We must win them. Above all, we must pray for them. Some are already in positions of authority in the Church. Others are yet among those waiting to receive an invitation to come to Christ. But wherever they are, they must be reached and trained to become effective disciples of our Lord.

BEGIN WITH A FEW

We should not expect a great number to begin with, nor should we desire it. The best work is always done with a few. Better to give a year or so to one or two men who learn what it means to conquer for Christ than to spend a lifetime with a congregation just keeping the program going. Nor does it matter how small or inauspicious the beginning may be; what counts is that those to whom we do give priority upon our life learn to give it away.

STAY TOGETHER

The only realistic way to effect this is by being together. If our followers are to see through us what they are to become, we must be with them. This is the essence of the plan—to let them see us in action so as to feel our vision and to know how it relates to daily experience. Evangelism thus becomes to them an intimately practical thing that has ramifications in everything else. It is seen as a way of life, not a theological dogma. What is more, by being with us, their own involvement in the work is inevitable.

GIVE THEM TIME

A plan like this, of course, is going to take time. Anything worthwhile does. But with a little forethought we can plan to do many things together which we would have to do anyway, such as visitation, going to conferences, getting recreation, and even having devotions together. Thus the time it takes to be together need not be overbearing. Likewise, if we are alert, most of the time our disciples could be with us while we are serving others, and in fact, helping us in our larger outreach.

GROUP MEETINGS

In order to give a little stability to this system, however, it may be necessary to arrange special times when the group, or part of it, can meet together with us. During these informal gatherings we can study the Bible, pray, and in general share with one another our deepest burdens and desires. It is not necessary to broadcast what is being done, or even at first to tell the group what our ultimate plan is, but just let the meetings grow out of the common need for fellowship. In turn the group can work out its own particular discipline within the framework of the Church.

This group idea is being rediscovered in many places today. As such it probably represents one of the most hopeful signs of awakening on the horizon. In all walks of life and within every kind of church connection little spiritual organisms are springing up, some of them struggling for direction, some off on a tangent, but on the whole, the movement expressing a deep yearning in the heart of men for the realities of Christian experience. Since they are not bound by tradition or fixed rules from without, there naturally is a wide difference in the emphasis and form these cells take, but the principle of close, disciplined fellowship within the group is common to most. It is this principle at the center which makes the method so conducive to growth, and for that reason all of us would do well to utilize it in our ministry with men.[1]

In this connection, it is not without great significance that the leading evangelist in the world today, Billy Graham, recognizes the tremendous potential of this plan when employed properly in the church. In response to the question, "If you were a pastor of a large church in a principle city, what would be your plan of action?" Mr. Graham replied: "I think one of the first things I would do would be to get a small group of eight or ten or twelve men around me that would meet a few hours a week and

1. There is no want of information relative to this movement, including the function and organization of groups. One needs to be discerning in reading this material, for much of it has a very shallow theological orientation. Still we dare not let this distract our interest in the idea itself. For practical suggestions along this line, the following recent books could be read with profit: Harry C. Munro, *Fellowship Evangelism Through Church Groups* (St. Louis: Bethany Press, 1951); Harold Wiley Freer and Francis B. Hall, *Two or Three Together* (New York: Harper & Brothers, 1954); John Casteel, *Spiritual Renewal Through Personal Groups* (New York: Association Press, 1957); Paul Miller, *Group Dynamics in Evangelism* (Scottdale, Penn.: Harold Press, 1958); Robert A. Raines, *New Life in the Church* (New York: Harper & Brothers, 1961); and Samuel M. Shoemaker, *With the Holy Spirit and With Fire* (New York: Harper & Brothers, 1960).

pay the price! It would cost them something in time and
effort. I would share with them everything I have, over a
period of years. Then I would actually have twelve
ministers among the laymen who in turn could take eight
or ten or twelve more and teach them. I know one or two
churches that are doing that, and it is revolutionizing the
church. Christ, I think, set the pattern. He spent most of
His time with twelve men. He didn't spend it with a
great crowd. In fact, every time He had a great crowd it
seems to me that there weren't too many results. The
great results, it seems to me, came in His personal
interview and in the time He spent with His twelve."[1]
Here Mr. Graham is merely echoing the wisdom of
Jesus' method.

EXPECT SOMETHING FROM THEM

But it is not enough just to involve persons in some
kind of group association, of which the Church is but the
larger expression. They must be given some way to
express the things which they have learned. Unless
opportunity is provided for this outreach, the group can
stagnate in self-contentment, and eventually fossilize into
nothing more than a mutual admiration society. We must
keep our purpose clear. The times that we come apart
from the world are not a release from the conflict, but
only a strategic maneuver to gain more strength for the
attack.

It is our business, then, to see to it that those with us
are given something to do which requires the best that is

1. Billy Graham, "Billy Graham Speaks: The Evangelical World
Prospect," an exclusive interview in *Christianity Today*, Vol. III, No.
1, October 13, 1958, p. 5. Used by permission.

in them. Everyone can do something.[1] First assignments might be normal, routine tasks, such as mailing letters, setting up a public address system for an outdoor service, or for that matter, merely letting them provide for our entertainment in their home. But gradually these responsibilities can be increased as they are able to do more. Those with a teaching gift could be utilized in the Sunday School. Before long we might conveniently assign them some pastoral work suited to their ability. Most anyone can call on the sick or visit in the hospital. Some might be encouraged to take over some speaking engagements or fill nearby pulpits. And, of course, everyone needs to be given some specific work by way of personal evangelism.[2]

---

1. Much has been said in recent years about the recovery of the lay ministry, but no book puts the issue any better than that of Paul Rees, *Stir up the Gift* (Grand Rapids: Zondervan, 1952). Other forthright applications of this idea can be found in J. E. Conant, *Every Member Evangelism* (New York: Harper & Brothers, 1922); Tom Allan, *The Face of My Parish* (New York: Harper & Brothers, 1953); Elton Trueblood, *The Company of the Committed* (New York: Harper & Brothers, 1961); and the thrilling missionary story of *Evangelism-in-Depth* (Chicago: Moody Press, 1961). A related work, written from the standpoint of missions, which has had a great impact since it first appeared a generation ago is the book by Roland Allen, *Missionary Methods: St. Paul's or Ours* (London: World Dominion Press, 1953), and its companion volume, *The Spontaneous Expansion of the Church* (London: World Dominion Press, 1949).

2. The materials dealing with methods of personal evangelism are plentiful and generally accessible. As one might expect, they do not all reflect the same quality, but this is a judgment which each student must make for himself. Since there are so many different ways to approach this subject, it would be helpful to read the counsel of several different men that have written in the field, among them: Arthur Archibald, Dawson Bryan, Robert H. Belton, S. L. Brengel, Shelby Carlett, J. Wilbur Chapman, Percy Crawford, David Dawson, Horace F. Dean, Gaines I. Dobbins, Murray W. Downey, Howard Ellis, William Evans, Leroy Gager, Gene Edwards, Albert F. Harper,

Probably no more essential contribution can they make to the ministry of the church than in the area of follow-up of new Christians.[1] Here, they can fill an indispensable role of the ministry by getting with those who are still babes in Christ and leading them on in the same disciplines and in the same way that they have been taught. Those whom we train for this work thus become the key to the preservation of every evangelistic effort of the church,[2] not only in conserving the forward advance, but also in assuring its continuing outreach.

Elmer Kauffman, Phillips Henderson, E. M. Harrison, Lionel Hunt, Nate Krupp, A. W. Knock, Florence Kee, Oscar Lowry, C. S. Lovett, J. C. Maculay, H. S. Miller, Roscoe Pershall, Rosalind Rinker, Stephen F. Olford, John A. O'Brien, Percy O. Ruoff, J. O. Sanders, Lorne C. Sanny, L. R. Scarborough, John T. Sisemore, Edgar J. Smith, Charles H. Spurgeon, John S. Stamm, Dimmock Steeves, G. Ernest Thomas, D. P. Thomson, R. A. Torrey, Charles G. Trumbull, H. Clay Trumbull, Orville S. Walters, Alonzo F. Wearner, F. D. Whitesell, S. A. Witmer, and Walter L. Wilson. This list is by no means complete, but at least it suggests that there is no reason for anyone to be denied the opportunity of getting more information.

1. Practical help in follow-up may be found in Arthur C. Archibald, *Establishing the Converts* (Philadelphia: Judson Press, 1952); Lorne C. Sanny, *The Art of Personal Witnessing* (Lincoln, Nebraska: Back to the Bible Publications, 1957); Sidney Powell, *Where Are the Converts* (Nashville: Broadmans Press, 1958); and especially the book by Waylon B. Moore, *New Testament Follow-up for Pastors and Laymen* (Grand Rapids: Wm. B. Eerdmans, 1963).

2. As in the case of personal work, there has also been a great deal written in the practical field of Church evangelism. C. E. Aturey, Arthur Archibald, Jesse Bader, J. N. Barnette, Andrew Blackwood, Theron Chastain, Kenneth Cole, J. E. Conant, Wildon Crossland, C. Lloyd Daughery, Eugene Golay, Charles L. Goodell, Byron Green, W. E. Grendstaff, Roland G. Leavell, William B. Riley, W. E. Sangster, Samuel A. Shoemaker, Roy H. Short, and John S. Stam are among some of the authorities that might be consulted. For a fairly comprehensive review of the many facets of the work in the church, probably as good a statement as any is the volume by George E. Sweazey, *Effective Evangelism* (New York: Harper & Brothers, 1953).

KEEP THEM GOING

All of this is going to require a lot of supervision, both in the personal development of these men, and in their work with others. We will have to make it a practice to meet with them and hear how things are going. This will mean seeking them out where they are or counseling with them while they are with us in other activity. Questions which have arisen in their experience must be answered while the circumstances that occasioned the problem are still fresh in their mind. Carnal attitudes and reactions need to be detected early and dealt with decisively, as also offensive personal habits, unfounded prejudices, and anything else that would obstruct their priesthood with God and with man.

The main thing is to help them keep growing in grace and in knowledge. It might be wise in respect to our human memory to set up for ourself a schedule of things to cover in the course of their training, and then to keep a record somewhere of their progress to be sure that nothing is left out. This is particularly necessary where we may be working with several at the same time, with each man at a different level of experience. We will need to exercise patience, for their development very likely will be slow and encumbered with many setbacks. But as long as they are honestly seeking to know the truth, and are willing to follow it, they will someday grow up to maturity in Christ.

HELP THEM CARRY THEIR BURDENS

What perhaps is the most difficult part of the whole process of training is that we must anticipate their problems and prepare them for what they will face. This is terribly hard to do, and it can become exasperating. It means that we can seldom put them out of our mind. Even when we are in our private meditations and study our disciples will still be in our prayers and dreams. But would a parent who loves his children want it any other way? We have to accept the burden of their immaturity until such time as they can do it for themselves. To take the attitude, at least in the early stages of their development, that they can handle completely on their own whatever comes along is inviting disaster. We must be sensible. As their guardian and advisor we are responsible for teaching our spiritual children how to live for the Master.

LET THEM CARRY ON

Everything should be leading these chosen men to the day when they will assume by themselves a ministry in their own sphere of influence. As that time approaches each one should be well along in his own training program with those won to Christ by his witness or who have been assigned to him for follow-up. Our strategy thus without their knowledge will have already been infused into their practice. However, not to leave it obscure, before withdrawing our supervision we should explain to them explicitly what has been our plan from the beginning. They need to have it clearly in mind so that they can measure their lives by it and also impart it to those that they are seeking to help.

SPIRITUAL EXPERIENCE ABOVE ALL

The crucial thing, of course, is their own spiritual experience. Before they should be turned loose from our control they need to be thoroughly established in the faith that overcomes the world. The devil, assisted by all the demons of Hell, will seek to defeat them by every cunning device at his command. The world to which they are going lies under his evil spell. It will be a battle all the way. Every inch of progress will have to be won by conquest, for the enemy will never surrender. Nothing less than the infilling of the Spirit of Christ will be sufficient to meet the challenge. Unless they live in His communion, and go forth in His purity and power, they can easily be overwhelmed by the forces amassed against them, and all our work with them be nullified.

Everything that we have done then depends upon the faithfulness of these men. It does not matter how many we enlist for the cause, but how many conquer for Christ. That is why all along our emphasis must be upon quality of life. If we get the right quality of leadership, the rest will follow; if we do not get it, the rest have nothing worth following.

THE PRICE OF VICTORY COMES HIGH

Such a high standard of expectation is costly, to be sure. Probably many of those we start out with will think it too much and fall by the way. We might as well face it now. Christian service is demanding, and if men are going to be of any use for God, they must learn to seek first the Kingdom. Yes, there will be disappointments. But of those who do come through, and go out to project our life into harvest fields beyond reckoning, there will be increasing joy as the years go by.

We are not living primarily for the present. Our satisfaction is in knowing that in generations to come our witness for Christ will still be bearing fruit through them in an ever-widening cycle of reproduction to the ends of the earth and unto the end of time.

IS THIS YOUR VISION?

The world is desperately seeking someone to follow. That they will follow someone is certain, but will he be a man who knows the way of Christ, or will he be one like themselves leading them only on into greater darkness?

This is the decisive question of our plan of life. The relevance of all that we do waits upon its verdict, and in turn, the destiny of the multitudes hangs in the balance.

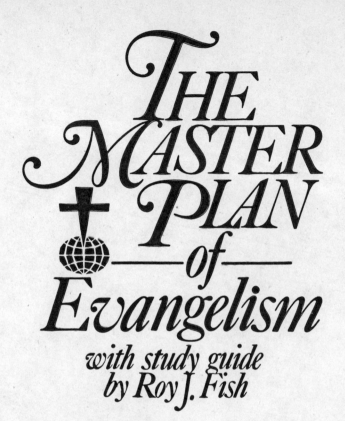

THE MASTER PLAN of Evangelism

with study guide
by Roy J. Fish

Introduction

One of the critical issues facing evangelical Christians in today's world has to do with an overall strategy of evangelism. The basic objective of this STUDY GUIDE is to assist you in discovering the evangelistic strategy of Jesus as set forth in the New Testament and as interpreted in the book, *The Master Plan of Evangelism* by Robert E. Coleman. The central goals of the STUDY GUIDE are as follows:

(1) To encourage exploration of the Gospels in search of Jesus' strategy.
(2) To review the meaning and values of the principles set forth by Him.
(3) To lead to a deeper commitment to His plan.
(4) To lead to an implementation of His strategy in our lives.

As to how the STUDY GUIDE can be most effectively used, two suggestions might be of help. First the STUDY GUIDE is designed for you to write in, so study it with a pencil in hand. Second, have a New Testament near for handy reference.

The STUDY GUIDE is composed of thirteen lessons. Each lesson will be similar in outline. First, there will be a brief summary of the content of the chapter or particular section of *The Master Plan* which is to be studied. This section will set forth the central idea or main thrust of the chapter and will call attention to basic learning goals for the chapter. Following will be a section called "Learning Procedures" which will contain questions which are designed to lead one to search out the major contents of a chapter. Only one chapter at a time should be done and, if possible, enough time set aside for the completion of the lesson at one sitting. Answers to questions, where needed, will be found at the end of the book.

This section is followed by suggestions for group discussion and group activities. As groups study the GUIDE, it will be helpful if each member answers the questions in the Learning Procedures before the group meets.

The ultimate objective of the study is the implementation of the Master Plan in the life of the reader. For this reason, each lesson will suggest some achievement goals and procedures which encourage personal application of the strategy of Jesus. Concluding each chapter is a brief section which offers ideas for further research of material appropriate for that chapter. A complete bibliography is given in the back of the book.

This STUDY GUIDE is sent forth with the prayer that your life will be richly blessed by it and that it will be of assistance to you in discovering and implementing the plan of the Master for your own life.

Roy J. Fish

The Master and His Plan

There seems to be renewed interest in the church today toward obeying the Great Commission of our Lord. Accompanying this concern, a great deal of thought is being given to new and creative methods of evangelism. But along with quickened interest and creativity in methods, there comes an imperative regarding another matter which is even more vital. This imperative has to do with strategy, and more particularly with restudying the basic evangelistic strategy of Jesus Himself.

That Jesus moved on earth with a deliberate strategy of evangelism is a fact about which there can be little question. He kept clearly before Him the fact that He had come "to seek and to save that which was lost" (Luke 19:10). He ordered His life by this objective. All Jesus ever said or did was a part of the divine strategy of evangelism for Him. But the concept the church of today must never overlook is that *as He was executing His plan, He was also setting forth a strategy of evangelism for His Church for all time.*

Consequently, it is not the task of the church to invent a *new* strategy. Our task is to *rediscover* His and to get in step with it. There is abundant evidence that the following of past traditions and the conformity to present religious culture have kept many churches from capturing His concept of strategy. When we do catch sight of it, it proves to be so different that its implications are nothing short of revolutionary. But for His best blessings to be on our efforts in evangelism, we must approximate the plan of the Master as nearly as possible. It must be done, even at the price of jettisoning some unnecessary religious activities and of altering some sacred organizational structures.

Learning Procedures

1. For approximately sixty seconds, look at the table of contents of *The Master Plan of Evangelism*. Listed below are the chapter headings in mixed order. After you have studied the proper order, see if you can arrange them correctly. Check the table of contents and compare your order with it.

   Supervision   _____
   Delegation   _____
   Selection   _____
   Association   _____
   Consecration   _____
   Reproduction   _____
   Impartation   _____
   Demonstration   _____

2. On page 11, the author speaks of "the evangelistic activity of the church." Write below your definition of evangelism.

   _____
   _____
   _____

3. When Dr. Coleman employs the word *strategy*, which of the three words below is most similar to what he means? Put a check in front of it
   _____Objectives   _____Methods   _____Principles

4. The best textbook on evangelism in print is

   _____

5. Answer the following true-or-false questions by writing T or
    F in the blank space which corresponds to the question.

    _____ (a) Jesus made a clear distinction between home
                  and foreign missions.
    _____ (b) The eight steps of guiding principles of Jesus
                  to train men come invariably in a deliberately
                  planned sequence.
    _____ (c) Method and strategy in evangelism are essen-
                  tially the same thing.

Group Discussion and Activity

Group discussion will center around four closely related
questions. They should be discussed in the order in which they
are found here.

(1) Discuss the primary objective for a church according to
     Jesus. Look at the Great Commissions found in Matthew
     28:19, John 20:21, and Acts 1:8.
(2) Take an objective look at your church or Christian group
     and compare the objectives of your church or group to
     His.
(3) Then ask: Is the organization and activity of our church
     or group really set up to achieve the basic objectives of
     Jesus?
(4) What changes could be made so that your church or
     group will more nearly approximate the objectives of our
     Lord?

Achievement Goals

At the outset of this study, test yourself as to past achievement
in evangelism:

(1) I tell other people about Christ with a view to win them to Him

frequently_____

sometimes_____

seldom_____

never_____

(2) I attempt to assist believers in becoming more mature in their Christian lives

frequently_____

sometimes_____

seldom_____

never_____

(3) Ask yourself: Do I have a strategy of evangelism for my own life? If not, am I willing to become a part of His?

Ideas for Further Research

1. A series of four cassette tapes by D. James Kennedy of Coral Ridge Presbyterian Church in Fort Lauderdale, Florida, are extremely helpful for this entire study. They are produced by David C. Cook Publishing Company, Elgin, Illinois. Tape #1 is particularly appropriate for this chapter.

2. The film, *Charlie Churchman and the Church Week*, Gospel Films, Muskegon, Michigan 49440, is a pointed caricature of busy Christians who are really doing nothing to fulfill the real mission of the church.

Selection

In considering the Master's plan, one cannot help but be struck by its simplicity. It is best described by the phrase "concentration upon a few." Its beginning was very unobtrusive as Jesus called a handful of men merely to follow Him. One is hardly impressed with the outward qualifications of the small group. They were rather common, to say the least, but they were teachable. And it was on this small group that Jesus concentrated His earthly ministry.

It should not be thought for a minute that Jesus completely neglected the many for the purpose of ministry to the few. The vision of the multitudes was always before Him and frequently the Gospel records make reference to His ministry to the masses. But Jesus was wise enough to see that before the multitudes could be permanently helped, they would need more personal care than He alone could give. His real hope of ministry to them lay in training a small group who could later lead the multitudes in the things of God.

The pattern of Jesus should teach us that the first duty of a spiritual leader is to lay a foundation upon which an evangelistic ministry can be built. Laying such a foundation will require concentration of effort on the time and talents of a few. Though the obvious results of such a plan will likely be slower in coming and probably unnoticed by most, the amount of good done and the number of people reached will ultimately be far greater.

Learning Procedures

1. Of the three answers to each of the questions listed below, circle the one which is correct.

    (a) Most of the disciples came from Galilee. The only one who seems to have come from Judea was: Thomas, Judas, Peter.

    (b) The total number of devoted followers of Jesus at the time of His death was around: 100, 500, 10,000.

    (c) Within the select apostolic group, three seemed to enjoy a more special relationship to the Master. One of them was: Andrew, Matthew, John.

2. Fill in the blank spaces of the sentences below with the correct words. Use the text to find them.

    (a) Jesus' concern was not with _____ to reach the multitudes, but with _____ whom the multitudes would follow.

    (b) The initial objective of Jesus' plan was _____ and after He returned to the Father.

    (c) The men called by Jesus are described by the author as being _____, _____, _____, and having all the _____ of their environment.

    (d) One can not transform a _____ except as _____ in the world are _____, and _____ can not be changed except as they are molded in the hands of the Master.

3. Answer the following true-or-false questions by writing T or F in the blank space in front of the question.

    ____ (a) In giving so much time to the twelve, Jesus demonstrated unconcern for the masses.

    ____ (b) Jesus' call to the twelve to follow Him made immediate impact upon the religious life of His day.

_____ (c) The word which best describes the basic principles of Jesus in his ministry to those He intended
to use is concentration.

Group Discussion and Activity

1. Look up the Scripture passage II Timothy 2:2. Discuss its
similarity to the principle employed by Jesus. Draw a
diagram to illustrate the principle.

Paul→Timothy→Faithful Men→Others

2. On page 31, Dr. Coleman states that, if one were to
"measure the effectiveness of His evangelism by the number of converts, Jesus doubtless would not be considered
among the most productive mass evangelists of the church."
If this is true, in what sense can we consider Jesus a great
evangelist? After discussion, read the section, "His Strategy," pages 31–33.

3. Discuss possible objections to the principle of concentration
on the few.

4. Discuss the sentence, "In an age when facilities for rapid
communication of the Gospel are available to the church as
never before, we are actually accomplishing less in winning
the world for God than before the invention of the horseless
carriage."

Achievement Goals

1. Make a list of possible opportunities of association which
you might have with a new or immature Christian. Some
will be readymade, i.e., a Sunday School teacher with his
class; or if you are a deacon, elder, or steward, perhaps you
are responsible for certain members. Other opportunities
will need to be planned.

2. Ask God to lead you to at least one person with whom you can work and lead to a life of discipleship.

3. Determine what requirements you will look for in the person.

_____   _____

_____   _____

4. List some things you want to see accomplished in this person's life.

_____   _____

_____   _____

_____   _____

Ideas for Further Research

1. For further reading material related to this chapter, the following would be helpful. (See bibliography for complete information on suggested books.)

   (a) Chapters one and two in the book, *Pastor Pastorum* by Henry Latham.

   (b) Chapter one of the book, *The Men Whom Jesus Made* by W. MacKintosh Mackay.

   (c) The chapter entitled, "Characteristics of His Pupils," in the book, *Jesus the Teacher* by J. M. Price.

   (d) Part three of the book, *The Apostles of Our Lord* by J. G. Greenbough.

2. Tape #2 of the Kennedy cassettes, mentioned in Lesson One, deals with the manner in which a contemporary church selects people for ministry.

LESSON 3

Association

The essence of the training program of Jesus was simply having His disciples with Him. To train men for world conquest He just drew them close to Himself. They learned first by association with Him. Jesus knew that in His presence His followers could learn what they really needed to know. It should be no surprise then that as the ministry of Jesus lengthened into its second and third years, He gave an increased amount of time to the twelve. Almost everything Jesus is recorded as having done, He did in the presence of at least some of his disciples. *He was building men through being with them.*

The church today has been slow to come to grips with this principle. Efforts by mature Christians at follow-up for the maturing of believers have lacked the aspect of personal attention needed by immature Christians. As a result of slipshod methods of follow-up, about 50 percent of those who unite with local churches eventually become inactive. The attempt has been made to produce disciples on an assembly-line basis and the results have been disastrous. Some system must be found whereby every new Christian may be taken under the wing of a mature believer and encouraged to stay there until he has matured to the point of leading another. To train people for this follow-up ministry is a current imperative facing every church which does not already have such a program.

Learning Procedures

1. To illustrate the point of association of the disciples with Jesus, the eighth and ninth chapters of Luke show at least a dozen experiences where the disciples were with Him. In at least eight of these they had opportunity to observe Him as He worked. List them below.

   _____
   _____
   _____
   _____
   _____
   _____
   _____
   _____

2. Fill in the blank spaces with correct answers.
   (a) The essence of the training program of Jesus was ___
   _____ .
   (b) Knowledge was gained by _____ before it was understood by _____ .
   (c) Three other illustrations of follow-up, over and above the twelve, were _____ , _____ , and _____ .

3. Circle the correct answer in the following questions.
   (a) During the second and third years of His ministry, Jesus gave (more) (less) time to the twelve.
   (b) Approximately (⅕) (⅓) (½) of the people who join a local church ultimately fall away.
   (c) All ten of the resurrection appearances of Jesus were to (unbelievers, that they might believe) (the disciples and Jewish leaders) (the disciples only).

Group Discussion and Activity

1. Secure the figure representing the total membership of your church or group. Then discuss the following:

(a) How many of our members attend Bible study or Sunday School?
(b) What percentage are faithful to the worship services?
(c) How many attend prayer meetings?
(d) How many are involved in some kind of Christian ministry?
(e) If the small percentages impress you, discuss the question: Why so few?

2. Suppose you are a member of a church or Christian organization which does not have people who are capable and committed to leading others to maturity. How should you proceed?

Achievement Goals

1. After you have chosen a person with whom to work, at what date will you make initial contact with the person?

2. How frequently will you attempt to be with the person?

3. What will be your first step in ministry to this person?

Ideas for Further Research

1. Many tapes from the Foundation Library, 435 W. Boyd, Norman, Oklahoma 73069, are appropriate for this and other chapters. A catalog may be ordered from the above address.
2. Further helpful reading will be found in the books:
(a) *New Testament Follow-up*, by Waylon B. Moore, pages 23–32.
(b) *Jesus the Teacher*, by J.M. Price, pages 46–60.

Consecration

Jesus' first requirement of His followers was a *willingness to obey Him*. Without a doubt some of them were brilliant men, but brilliance was not one of our Lord's stipulations. The one thing our Lord insisted on was loyalty to Him. Jesus continued to insist on this even when loyalty became increasingly difficult. He always claimed the right of setting forth the conditions and terms for being His disciple. But the fact that the disciples saw in Him the spirit of obedience on which He insisted challenged them to stay with Him.

Jesus knew that increased knowledge comes through obedience. He saw that learning truths about Him would come in time, if only the disciples were willing to obey. One cannot be a leader who has not first learned to be a follower. He knew that development of character and purpose would come only through obedience. This is why He was willing to endure patiently many of their human failings as long as they were willing to obey Him.

There is a critical need in the church today for a new commitment to the Lordship of Christ. Stressing obedience at any cost must once again characterize the revolutionary message of the church. The people of God—preachers and layman alike—must cease to be complacent toward the commands of Christ. It is a situation which *must* be remedied. It may be that churches will have to begin a program of effective evangelism through a committed few who draw a small number of people to themselves and instill into this group the real meaning of obedience to Christ. Such action will be at least a start.

Learning Procedures

1. In Luke 9:57–62, three men came to Jesus as prospective followers. In your own words, describe the answer of Jesus to each. Then check pages 52–53.

   (a) _____

   (b) _____

   (c) _____

   _____

2. (a) What is your definition of a "disciple"?_____

   _____

   (b) What is Dr. Coleman's definition of the word?

   _____

3. What is the basic proof of real love for Christ?

   _____

4. "It must be remembered too that Jesus was making men to lead His church in conquest, and no one can ever be a _____ until first he has learned to _____ a leader."

5. Three specific conditions for discipleship are mentioned in the Gospel of John. List them below as you look up the Scripture verse.

   (a) John 8:31 _____

   (b) John 13:35 _____

   (c) John 15:8 _____

6. Jesus is to be Lord of every part of the life of a Christian. Listed below are some areas of the Christian life. Match them with the Scripture passage.

   _____Possessions   A. Psalm 19:14

   _____Time   B. Matthew 6:19–21

   _____Speech   C. Colossians 3:18–21

   _____Thought Life   D. Ephesians 5:15–16

   _____Family Life   E. Philippians 4:8

Group Discussion and Activity

1. Discuss the meaning of the word "consecration." Then call to memory as many New Testament instances as you can where consecration is exemplified.
2. Think over your knowledge of Christian acquaintances and see of you can find consecration exemplified in some of them.
3. On page 57 of the text, the author lists several passages which reflect Jesus' commitment to the will of God.

   John 4:34; John 5:30; John 15:10; Luke 22:42.
   Discuss what these meant to Jesus.

4. How does the Lordship of Christ in one's life relate to witnessing?
5. If there is a widespread indifference to Christ among your Christian acquaintances, how can you proceed to alter this situation?
6. Distribute five pipe cleaners to each person present. Then ask each person to think about his Christian life. Ask each one to take the five pipe cleaners and twist and mold them into what he believes to be the best description of his Christian life. Take about five minutes to do this. Then let each person share with the group the meanings he has twisted into the pipe cleaners.

Achievement Goals

1. What does Jesus expect of me as a disciple? _____
   _____
2. The three passages listed below represent commands of Jesus to His followers. Read them and rate yourself on the chart below.

   John 5:39   Luke 18:1   Matthew 4:19

I am obedient to these commands:
consistently_____
most of the time_____
some of the time_____
seldom_____
never_____

3. Check yourself.
I seldom bear witness for Christ to others because:

_____ I am afraid I will offend someone.
_____ I am afraid the person will refuse to accept Christ.
_____ My life is not consistent as a Christian.
_____ I really do not think it is my job to do it.
_____ I am afraid questions would be asked which I could not answer.
_____ I am not really sure others need Christ.
_____ I am not sure I have a real and vital relationship with Christ myself.

4. If you sense a need to do so, pause here and take time to pray a prayer of commitment to God relative to the above commands. Perhaps this prayer will reflect your feelings:

O God, I confess that I have not been obedient to the commands of Christ as I should. Right now I commit myself to You anew, trusting You to so work in my life that I will be consistent in my study of Your Word, in my prayer life, and in sharing the Good News of Jesus with others. Amen.

5. Describe below your plans for future provisions for personal Bible study and prayer.

_____
_____
_____

6. If you know Christian friends who seem to be uninterested in obedience to Christ, here are some ways you might help them.

    (a) Resolve to pray for them. "I will pray for the following Christians to grow in their devotion to Christ:

        _____

        _____

        _____."

    (b) Cultivate a closer acquaintance with them, resolving, "I will cultivate a closer acquaintance with the following and endeavor to lead them into a deeper Christian life:

        _____

        _____

        _____."

Ideas for Further Research

1. Films:
       (a) The film, *In His Steps*, produced by Ken Anderson Films, based on the famous novel of the same name, is a contemporary challenge to consecration.
       (b) For teenagers, a series of filmstrips is published by Family Films, 2900 Queen Lane, Philadelphia, Pennsylvania 19129, entitled *Christian Teen-agers Spiritual Life Kit*.
2. A large number of books deal with this subject. One classic which every Christian should read is *The Christian's Secret of a Happy Life* by Hannah Whitall Smith.
3. There are several series of Bible study booklets which are helpful in leading one to profitable study of the Scriptures. Some of them are:
       (a) *Ten Basic Steps Toward Christian Maturity*, Campus Crusade for Christ, Inc., Arrowhead Springs, San Bernadino, California.

(b) *Studies in Christian Living*, The Navigators, Colorado Springs, Colorado 80900.

(c) Set of six *Win* or *Grow Booklets*, Sunday School Board of the Southern Baptist Convention, Nashville, Tennessee.

Impartation

The disciples could not help but be impressed with the fact that Jesus' life was a *life of giving*. He reflected the supreme demonstration of love as He literally gave his life away. They were constantly impressed that He loved a lost world. Jesus both understood and attempted to convey to them that He had been set apart for the evangelistic end of giving His life for the world's redemption. Through Jesus' demonstration, the disciples learned what real consecration meant. The fact that they learned self-giving was to be a factor by which the multitudes were to be convinced of the reality of the Gospel.

But the twelve could never exhibit this kind of love apart from the impartation of Jesus' own life to them. This He did when He sent the Holy Spirit to indwell their lives. In giving the Holy Spirit to His followers, Jesus was also equipping them for evangelistic ministry. He frequently reiterated the fact that evangelism was not a human undertaking but a work of the Holy Spirit. His last hours with the twelve were spent assuring them that the Holy Spirit would be adequate equipment for the evangelistic task. Thus it was that Pentecost was an absolute necessity before His followers could live, love, and serve in the ministry of evangelism.

And so it is today. Jesus' followers must have His life through the indwelling Spirit if His work is to be accomplished in and through the church. Only then will we be properly motivated. Only then will we possess the power to make Him known. Only then will we demonstrate the self-sacrificing spirit necessary to effective evangelism.

Learning Procedures

1. Obedience is more than keeping laws. It is _____
    _____ .

2. Jesus' constant renewal of His consecration to God expressed itself in _____

3. The primary purpose for which Jesus sanctified Himself was _____ .

4. Jesus was God in _____; but the Spirit was God in _____ .

5. Here is a comparison study of Jesus with the twelve. There were things cherished by the disciples which Jesus refused. On the other hand, there were things they sought to escape which He willingly accepted. Below are seven words. In the two columns, list those cherished by the twelve and the ones Jesus accepted willingly.

    physical satisfaction—poverty—humiliation
    prestige—death—popular acclaim—sorrow

Disciples	Jesus
_____	_____
_____	_____
_____	_____
	_____

6. List five things mentioned by our author which Jesus gave His followers:

    _____
    _____
    _____
    _____
    _____

Group Discussion and Activity

1. Discuss the meaning of the word "sanctification" as it is found in John 17:18, 19. Then check pages 63, 64 in the text.

2. If your group is large enough, divide into three small groups. Makes the following assignments:
   (a) Assign the first group to describe the work of the Holy Spirit in leading the Christian to be Christlike.
   (b) Assign the second group to describe the work of and the necessity of the Holy Spirit for effective evangelism.
   (c) Assign the third group to describe the conditions for the infilling with the Holy Spirit.
3. What one area in your life needs to be changed or strengthened in the light of today's study?

Achievement Goals

1. Get alone with God and make a list of every known sin or failure of which you are aware. Write them down, one by one, until everything the Holy Spirit has shown you to be wrong in your life is listed. Turn to 1 John 1:9 in your Bible. Confess the sins to God and write 1 John 1:9 across the sheet and destroy it.
2. In looking at your life, if you are aware of any area which has not been yielded to Christ, surrender that area of your life now.
3. Now pray the following prayer:

Dear Father,
I confess that there have been areas in my life which I have not yielded to You and as a result I have sinned against You. I thank You for complete forgiveness and right now yield every part of my life completely to You. By faith, I now claim the fullness of the Holy Spirit and thank You for taking control of my life and for filling me with Him.

Amen

Ideas for Further Research

1. A large number of tapes from The Foundation Library, mentioned in Lesson Three, deal with the subject of the Holy Spirit.
2. Many books have been written on the subject of the Holy Spirit. Two recent ones are *On Tiptoe with Joy!* by John T. Seamands, and *The Key to Triumphant Living*, by Jack R. Taylor.
3. The small pamphlet, *Have You Made the Wonderful Discovery of the Spirit-Filled Life?* published by Campus Crusade for Christ Inc., Arrowhead Springs, San Bernardino, California, is a helpful tool. A similar pamphlet may be obtained from the Evangelism Division of the Baptist General Convention of Texas, Dallas, Texas 75201, *How to Have a Spirit-Filled Life*.

LESSON 6

Demonstration

It was a deliberate part of the strategy of Jesus to demonstrate the kind of life He planned for His people to live. Thus, the twelve *observed in Him the life they were to live and teach.* Everything about Him was a demonstration for their sake and ours. He purposely let them see Him talking with His Father in prayer. They saw what it did for Him and yearned to know more of its power in their own lives. They were powerfully impressed with His mastery and use of the Old Testament Scriptures. Of particular importance is the fact that they watched as He won people to Himself. They learned as they watched Him practice before them what He wanted them to learn. Classes were always in session as the Master Teacher, in a natural manner, turned situation after situation into a learning opportunity.

Spiritual leaders are to emulate the plan of Jesus today. To effect this, we must be willing to demonstrate with our lives what we want others to learn. In order to accomplish this, we must be with those whom we want to lead. We must pray with them, help them in their study of the Scriptures, and take them with us as we attempt to win others to Christ. We will impart the way of life to others only as they see it in us. This is the Master's method and its implementation is a must if others are to be adequately trained to do His work.

Learning Procedures

1. Though Jesus' life was a constant demonstration of how to live, our author singles out three particular areas of dem-

onstration through which He wanted to teach the twelve. They were _____ , _____ , and _____ .

2. The Gospels call attention to Jesus' practice of prayer how many times?_____

3. "Altogether there are at least _____ references to the Old Testament in His dialogues with the disciples in the four Gospels, to say nothing of the more than _____ allusions to it in His speaking with others."

4. Jesus' example is indication to His followers that they should know the Scriptures. According to the following verses, how may the Scriptures help us in our lives today?
   (a) 1 Peter 2:2 _____
   _____
   (b) Psalm 119:105 _____
   _____
   (c) John 15:7 _____
   _____

5. What lessons can you learn from the prayer life of Jesus?
   (a) Matthew 14:23 _____
   _____
   (b) Mark 1:35 _____
   _____
   (c) Luke 6:12 _____
   _____

Group Discussion and Activity

1. Compare Jesus' attitude toward the Scriptures with the statement of Paul in 2 Timothy 3:16–17.
2. Discuss the implications of: 1 Corinthians 11:1; Philippians 3:17; 2 Timothy 1:13; and Philippians 4:9.
3. Role-playing is the unrehearsed, dramatic enactment of a human conflict situation by two or more persons for the purpose of analysis by the group. Employing the procedure

of role-playing, select three members of the group to role-play the following:

THE PROBLEM   Here is a new Christian who wants to grow in the Lord. He is finding it difficult to pray. He doesn't know how to study his Bible and his first attempt to win someone to Christ was a miserable failure.

Let one person act out failure in these three areas. A second person, representing a lost friend, will be needed to act out failure in winning someone to Christ. Then, let a third person, representing a mature Christian, show through demonstration how having someone to teach in these areas can be of invaluable assistance.

Achievement Goals

1. If you have been working with a person, decide in what way you are going to help teach this person to learn the following things:
    (a) How to pray
    (b) How to study the Bible effectively
    (c) How to share the Good News with others
    (d) How to be victorious in temptation
    (e) What to do when one sins

2. I spend about this much time in Bible study and prayer each week:

less than ½ hour	½ to 1 hour	1–2 hours	2–3 hours	more than 3 hours

3. Do you have a system of Scripture memory? If not, begin to commit at least one verse a week to memory.

Ideas for Further Research

1. A section of *Pastor Pastorum*, Latham, "The Schooling of the Apostles," pages 270–310, is a helpful study in demonstration.
2. The film, *Like a Mighty Army*, produced by Gospel Films Inc., of Muskegon, Michigan, is the story of the Coral Ridge Presbyterian Church of Fort Lauderdale, Florida. It strongly emphasizes the aspect of demonstration in teaching others to witness.
3. For assistance in memorizing Scripture verses, packets containing verses on cards may be obtained from The Navigators, Colorado Springs, Colorado 80900, and from the Billy Graham Evangelistic Association, Minneapolis, Minnesota 55440.

Delegation

During the first year of Jesus' ministry, the disciples did little more than watch Jesus work. Though they were assigned responsibilities from the first, their initial involvement was with tasks which were quite menial. But this was a part of the Master's method. First, He led them into a vital relationship with God; then He showed them how He worked, and *only then* did He share with them the extent of their responsibilities. But He was always working with them with an eye toward the time they would take over His ministry.

Finally, after more than a year of training, Jesus realized they were ready for evangelistic work of their own. But Jesus was careful to thoroughly instruct them before He sent them out. The instructions are of great significance, since in them Jesus outlined explicitly what He had been implicitly teaching from the start. It is of special importance to notice that Jesus told them to concentrate their work on the more promising individuals who could carry on the work after they had gone. With assurance that they could expect hardship, He sent them, two by two, on their mission.

Involvement in the evangelistic task is an absolute imperative for every true follower of our Lord. Work assignments should be given to those whom we are training. These assignments should be of a practical nature at first, but always given with a view to preparing those we are leading for direct involvement in the redemptive ministry of our Lord.

Learning Procedures

1. Before telling the disciples they were to engage in world evangelism, Jesus' method included _____

and _____ .

2. For a period of approximately _____ , the disciples did little more than watch Jesus work.

3. What is the author's explanation as to why Jesus said to the twelve, "Go not into the way of the Gentiles, and into any city of the Samaritans enter ye not: But go rather to the lost sheep of the house of Israel" (Matthew 10:5,6)?

_____
_____
_____

4. How does our author interpret the instruction of Jesus, "Into whatsoever city or village ye shall enter, search out who in it is worthy; and there abide till ye go forth"?

_____
_____
_____

5. What indication is there that the witnessing efforts of the twelve on their first mission were to some degree effective?

_____

6. With the text and a New Testament in hand, match the following:

_____Luke 24:44–47   A. "Make disciples"
_____John 20:19–24   B. "Thomas was not with them"
_____Matthew 28:19   C. Promise of the Holy Spirit
_____Acts 1:8   D. "Feed my sheep"
_____John 21:15–17   E. "Into all the world"
_____Mark 16:15   F. "Repentance should be preached"

Group Discussion and Activity

1. Discuss this paragraph:

    Christian disciples are sent men—sent out in the same
    work of world evangelism to which the Lord was sent, and
    for which He gave His life. Evangelism is not an optional
    accessory to our life. It is the heartbeat of all that we are
    called to be and do. It is the commission of the church
    which gives meaning to all else that is undertaken in the
    Name of Christ. With this purpose clearly in focus, every-
    thing which is done and said has glorious fulfillment of
    God's redemptive purpose—educational institutions, social
    programs, hospitals, church meetings of any kind—
    everything done in the Name of Christ has its justification
    in fulfilling this mission.

2. Discuss the words of Jesus in Matthew 10:34–38.

    Think not that I came to send peace on earth: I came
    not to send peace, but a sword. For I am come to set a
    man at variance against his father, and the daughter
    against her mother, and the daughter-in-law against her
    mother-in-law. And a man's foes shall be they of his own
    household. He that loveth father or mother more than
    me is not worthy of me: and he that loveth son or
    daughter more than me is not worthy of me. And he that
    taketh not his cross and followeth after me, is not worthy
    of me.

    Now look at Dr. Coleman's comment on pages 87–88.

3. Discuss the significance of the author's interpretation of
    Matthew 10:5, 6, as it relates to the beginning efforts of
    someone you might be training as a witness.

4. Look at the warnings of Jesus as to hardships the twelve might experience. Consider them in the light of the passages: 1 Peter 2:21; Philippians 1:29; and 2 Timothy 3:12.

Achievement Goals

1. List some work assignments you might assign to a new Christian with whom you are working.
2. If you have been working with a Christian in personal witnessing, let him begin to take over certain simpler parts of the conversation with a non-Christian.
3. Ask yourself the question, "Am I willing to witness for Jesus, even if it means bearing reproach for Christ's sake?"
4. If something seems to be hindering you from witnessing, check the list below. Be honest and face up to what it is. Trust God for continuous strength to overcome.

_____False priorities
_____Laziness
_____Fear
_____Prejudice against evangelism
_____Sins of the flesh
_____
_____
_____

Above all, make yourself *available* to God.

Ideas for Further Research

1. Books:
   (a) *Every Member Evangelism*, by J. E. Conant, is a powerful book encouraging delegation of the responsibility of witnessing.
   (b) A section of *The Training of the Twelve*, by A. B. Bruce, "First Attempts at Evangelism," pages 99–119, is very appropriate.

LESSON 8

Supervision

Though He had entrusted the twelve with some evangelistic responsibility, Jesus did not yet look on them as finished products who were ready to graduate. Even in the limited amount of redemptive work in which they had engaged, *they needed supervision*. Thus, Jesus got with them following their tours of service to hear their reports and to share with them His knowledge about difficulties they might have encountered or victories they might have won. And indeed, this is no isolated incident. Through constant fellowship with them, Jesus was perpetually keeping check on the twelve. Throughout His ministry with them, the experiences of the disciples, whether they represented success or failure, were raw materials for Jesus to use in teaching and making application. He was ever alert to their actions and reactions, keeping in mind that His supervision was one more step in equipping them for ministry. When He finally did leave them to go back to the Father, He promised the Holy Spirit to them to continue to supervise their work.

In equipping people for evangelistic ministry today, we cannot presume that merely showing people how will result in the work being done. Nor can we assume that the successful completion of one task reflects a readiness on the part of the person being trained to be on his own. Until disciples have been brought to a place of maturity, close supervision is still a necessity.

Learning Procedures

1. Compare the report session of the twelve with that of the seventy.

    _____

    _____

2. What was Jesus' reaction to the report of the seventy?

    _____

    _____

3. List one instance where Jesus used failure on the part of the twelve to bring out truth they needed to know.

    _____

4. The author uses three words to describe Jesus' plan of teaching. They are _____ , _____ , and _____ .

Group Discussion and Activity

1. The author uses the term "world conquest" twice in this chapter. What, in your opinion, is meant by this?

2. Discuss this paragraph:

    When will we learn the lessons of Christ not to be satisfied merely with the firstfruits of those who are sent out to witness? Disciples must be brought to maturity. There can be no substitute for total victory, and our field is the world. We have not been called to hold the fort, but to storm the heights. It is in this light that the final step in Jesus' strategy of evangelism can be understood.

3. Someone you have been working with has been rebuffed. It could be in one of several ways. Discuss how you could encourage him when he encounters the following:

    (a) On introducing himself, a door was slammed in his face.

    (b) On sharing the Good News, someone sincerely asked, "But how do you know it is really true?"

    (c) "I don't believe there is a God."

    (d) "Isn't Christian experience only psychological?"

4. Let this meeting be a report session. Ask and answer the following questions.

    (a) Who have you met this week that needs help?

    (b) What have you done about it?

    (c) Think of three people—family, friends, business associates, shut-ins, etc.—to whom you will demonstrate Christian concern this week. You will take a few minutes to share with them or will perform some planned act of kindness toward them. Record the act, whether done by phone, in person, or by letter. Write down what happened.

Achievement Goals

1. Have a planned report session after sending your friend out to do some piece of Christian work.
2. Make a list of discouraging difficulties a new witness might face and be prepared to help him with them.

_____ _____

_____ _____

Ideas for Further Research

1. Gospel Films has produced four Teaching Training Films on Lay Witnessing as it is done in the Coral Ridge Presbyterian Church, Fort Lauderdale, Florida. The third of these, *On the Job Training*, emphasizes this aspect of teaching.
2. The book, *Evangelism Explosion*, by D. James Kennedy, has a wholesome emphasis on supervision.

LESSON 9

Reproduction

The ultimate goal of Jesus for His disciples was that *His life be reproduced in them and through them into the lives of others.* The fact that the group of men He led was small made little difference. If they were adequately trained, they would produce lives which would be like theirs. Lives like these would produce the same kind of fruit until Jesus could envision the whole world hearing His message. The ultimate victory would come through their faithful witness of Him. His Gospel would conquer as they reproduced and taught their disciples to reproduce. Reproduction was our Lord's desire for the twelve but multiplication was the ultimate end.

Today, as then, the test of an evangelistic program is not the number of people who are being reached for first-time decisions. The real test is: *Are those who are being reached reaching others?* Is our fruit bearing fruit? Are we only making converts—or are we building leaders who can in turn build other leaders?

The early church, with its incorporation of the plan of winning and developing men to reproduce, proved the workability of Jesus' plan; but ensuing centuries witnessed the virtual abandonment of it for one of mass recruitment. *The need of the hour is a return to the kind of evangelism which majors in men winning other men to Christ and building those they have won into disciples who can win and build others.*

Learning Procedures

1. Answer the following true-or-false questions.

    _____ (a) Reproduction is the chief end of evangelism.

_____ (b) Mass recruitment by the church seems to have worked to the detriment of the Christian movement.

_____ (c) The principal of Jesus in evangelism has never been recaptured by the church to any great extent since the fourth century.

_____ (d) The only real command in Matthew 28:19-20 is to make disciples.

2. Matthew 9:36-38 pictures an experience of Jesus seeing vast multitudes of people. Describe his response to this.

_____

What did He encourage His disciples to pray?_____

_____

3. What is the ultimate evaluation of our life and witness as to the redemptive purposes of God?_____

_____

4. The test of any work of evangelism thus is not _____ _____ , but in _____ .

5. Similarly, the criteria upon which a church should measure its success are not _____ , nor_____ , but rather_____ .

6. Evangelism is not done by _____ but by _____ .

7. The new evangelism needed is not better methods but better_____ .

Group Discussion and Activity

1. Dr. Coleman speaks of Jesus' foreseeing the day "when the Gospel of salvation in His name would be proclaimed convincingly to every creature." Discuss the prospects for this happening in our generation.

2. Study thoroughly John 15:1-16. Note how many times the word *fruit* is used in these passages. Discuss what Jesus meant by this word. Then see page 108. Notice verse 16

where Jesus talks about fruit remaining. What is meant by this?

3. Discuss the paragraph on page 110:

    What really counts in the ultimate perpetuation of our work is the faithfulness with which our converts go out and make leaders out of their converts, not simply more followers. Surely we want to win our generation for Christ, and to do it now, but this is not enough. Our work is never finished until it has assured its continuation in the lives of those redeemed by the Evangel.

4. Discuss what you would do about winning the following people:

    (a) Next door there lives a man who would like for all churches to be destroyed. He is very open in his hostility to Christians and believes they are a detriment to society. Sometimes his hatred almost turns into a rage. What, if anything, could be done to reach him for Christ? Do you honestly believe he could be saved? Read Acts 8:3; 9:1–6.

    (b) Next door lives a man who is extremely religious. He prays, helps the poor, and leads his family to be religious, yet, he has never come to know Christ personally. What would your attitude toward him be? What would you do to reach this man for Christ? Do you believe he could become a Christian? Read Acts 10.

Achievement Goals

1. You have been working with a person with a view to leading that person to become a witness. As he goes with you, let him have more and more of the conversation until ultimately he carries it all the way, even to the point of asking a person to accept Christ. If the person with whom you have been working is not to this point, stay with him until he is.

The person with whom I am working is:

_____ able to enter into introductory conversation and introduce Christ into the conversation.

_____ able to share the Gospel intelligently, but not ready to ask for a commitment.

_____ able to share the Gospel and lead a person to a decision.

2. Your goal is not only to help the person with whom you have been working to lead someone to Christ. You have also been working toward his being able to take the person he has led to Christ and lead him to a place of maturity. Be sure the person with whom you have been working understands that at this point.

Ideas for Further Research

1. Several films have very poignant messages relative to the content of this chapter. Among them:

   (a) *No Time to Wait*, Augsburg Publishing House, 426 South Fifth Street, Minneapolis, Minnesota 55415.

   (b) *Born to Witness*, Family Films, 5823 Santa Monica Blvd., Hollywood, California 90038.

   (c) *The Gospel Blimp*, Gospel Films, Muskegon, Michigan 49440.

   (d) *How to Witness*, Broadman Films, Sunday School Board of the Southern Baptist Convention, Nashville, Tennessee.

   (e) Part I and Part II of the Coral Ridge teaching training films on Lay Witnessing: *Challenge to Witness* and *The Gospel Presentation*, Gospel Films.

2. Tapes #3 and #4 of the Coral Ridge Cassettes, David Cook Publishing Company, Elgin, Illinois, are extremely helpful here.

The Master and Your Plan—Step One

There is an old story, imagined by someone, of Jesus ascending back to Heaven and encountering the Angel Gabriel shortly after He arrived. Gabriel was terribly interested in what our Lord had been doing on earth. Jesus responded by explaining that while on earth, He had died on a cross to save men from their sins and had been raised up by God's power. He had now returned to Heaven to take His place at God's right hand to intercede for those whom He had come to save. Jesus concluded by saying that it was His desire that all men everywhere hear the message of what He had done for them. Gabriel asked, "And what is your plan for getting this done?" Our Lord responded, "I have left the message in the hands of a dozen or so men. I am trusting them to spread it everywhere." Somewhat surprised, Gabriel exclaimed, "Twelve men! And what if they fail?" Jesus is reported to have said, "I have no other plan."

Regardless of the imaginary aspect of it, the main point of the story is true. Jesus did leave the task of evangelizing in the hands of a small number of people. But they so thoroughly trained others to bear effective witness that soon large numbers of trained disciples were sharing the truth about Jesus all over Jerusalem, Judea, Samaria, Galilee, and ultimately to the uttermost parts of the earth.

His plan, revolving around trained disciples who are winning and training others to win and train, has never changed.

Learning Procedures

1. As you work with a person, list here some opportunities you might have of getting together with that person for training in discipleship.

   _____   _____

   _____   _____

   _____

2. In working with a person or a small group, what are some activities in which you might engage when you are together?

   _____   _____

   _____   _____

3. What are some possible assignments you might make to a person you are helping to disciple?

   (a) Early or first assignments.

   _____   _____

   _____   _____

   (b) Assignments to make as the person matures in the Lord.

   _____   _____

   _____   _____

4. At what time would you explain your strategy to a person with whom you have been working?

   _____

Group Activity and Discussion

1. Make this session a report session. Discuss: Whom have I met this week that needs help? What have I done to help someone this week? What was the response?
2. Discuss: "Better to give a year or so to one or two men who learn what it means to conquer for Christ than to spend a lifetime with a congregation just keeping the program

going." Ask the group to agree or disagree. What are the implications of this statement? What is involved in the phrase, "conquer for Christ"?

3. On page 125, Dr. Coleman speaks of some people who think the standards of discipleship are too high and fall by the way. Think of some in the New Testament who did. See Acts 1:25; I Timothy 4:10; II Timothy 1:15; II Timothy 1:19, 20. What will your response be if some with whom you are working prove to be unteachable, unwilling to pay the price, and fall by the way?

4. In your prayer period, as a group, pray for each person in the group by name.

Personal Achievement

1. Write out your own personal testimony about becoming a Christian in approximately 150–200 words. It should be outlined something like this: *First,* what your life without Christ was like. *Second,* how you became a Christian. *Third,* what life has been like since you received Christ. Steer away from heavy theological words and clichés which mean nothing to most people who are not Christians. Major on what Christ means to you and is doing for you today. Commit this to memory.

2. You are a Sunday School teacher. Each one in your class is a Christian and attends with some degree of regularity. You prepare lessons faithfully, visit absentees, and occasionally plan a party or outing for your class. As yet, nothing outstanding has happened in the lives of members of your class. How do you plan to proceed with the Master Plan? Look at the chapter headings again. Proceed on the basis of the contents of the chapter headings.

3. You are a part of the bus ministry of your church. A child who rides your bus makes a profession of faith. How will you go about your ministry of follow-up?

4. What are the primary lessons you have learned in the preceding nine chapters? How have you begun to put them into practice? What are your plans for the future?

Ideas for Further Research

1. Film IV of the Coral Ridge training series, *Follow-Up*, Gospel Films, Muskeegon, Michigan.
2. The book, *Evangelism Explosion*, by D. James Kennedy, has an excellent section on follow-up.
3. The pamphlet, *Christ in You*, published by Inter-Varsity Press, 1519 N. Astor, Chicago, Illinois 60610, is good material for follow-up of a new Christian.
4. The booklet, *How to Have a Quiet Time*, published by The Navigators, Colorado Springs, Colorado, is pertinent in follow-up.
5. A series of follow-up tapes may be obtained from the Coral Ridge Presbyterian Church, 1901 Northeast 50th Street, Fort Lauderdale, Florida.

The Master and Your Plan—Step Two

Recently I saw one of the most forceful demonstrations of the importance of spiritual multiplication I can remember. Two men were asked to come and stand at the front of a very crowded auditorium. Both of them represented pastors who win people to Christ through personal witnessing. One of the two (perhaps the more aggressive witness) represented the pastor who wins many people to Christ personally, but who is so busy winning people he never takes time to train anyone to do it. The other (perhaps less dynamic in his own personal evangelism) takes time to train those whom he wins to win others. He goes even one step further and trains them to train the ones they have won.

The demonstration began when each of the two men went out into the congregation and brought back with them to the front of the auditorium another person who represented someone they had won to Christ. The first pastor continued to do this, to bring them one by one, until after ten trips he had ten others with him at the front representing those he had won to Christ. The second pastor, who was training those he had won, went into the congregation along with the first person he had won and trained, and each of them brought back one. This made four. The four won to Christ and trained went out and each brought back one and there were eight. This man and those whom he had trained made only five trips into the congregation. But thirty-two people stood with him after five trips in contrast to the ten people who stood with the other. Had this pastor and those he trained made ten trips into the congregation, 1,024 people would have stood with him! The difference is the difference between addition and multiplication. *It is more important to train a soul winner than to win a soul.* The church must return to the principle of multiplication if we are to make the impact on this lost world our Lord would have us to make.

Learning Procedures

1. A number of concepts are included in spiritual growth which leads to maturity. Some of them are found in the verses below. Look at the verse and see if you can determine what the particular aspect of growth is.

   1 John 5:13_____

   Ephesians 4:14_____

   Ephesians 4:13_____

   Matthew 4:19_____

   Matthew 28:19_____

2. Here is one for those who love arithmetic. Suppose you were the only Christian in the world. In the next six months you win one person and train him to win and train others. At the end of six months there are two Christians, both capable of winning and training. Each of you wins and trains one in the next six months and then there are four. Each wins and trains one in the next six months and there are eight. Following this procedure, how many people would be won to Christ over a period of sixteen years? Don't lose heart in working it.

   Answer: _____

Group Discussion and Activity

1. Secure the number of people who were added to your church on profession of faith last year. Then secure the total

membership of your church. Divide the total number of people added by profession into the total membership. The quotient (figure which represents the answer) determines how many members it took to win one person to Christ and to an open confession of Him in your church last year.

2. Now, figure how many people would be won to Christ if every member won one person in the next year. What would your approximate membership be at the end of the year? If each of these won someone during the next year, how many would be won?

3. Bring some old newspapers with you to the group meeting. Think for a minute about someone who is away from God and whom you would like to see get right with God. Concentrate on what you believe his basic needs to be. What are his or her anxieties, his hang-ups, his tensions? Put yourself in his or her shoes. Take a few minutes and take the newspaper and tear out of it every headline, every ad, every picture, and everything that reminds you of your friend who is not right with God. Discard the remainder of the paper and using the materials you have torn out, describe your friend in two minutes to the rest of the group.

Personal Achievement

1. Read Ephesians 4:11, 12 in a modern translation of the New Testament. Paul makes it clear that evangelism is to be a part of the life of every member of Christ's church. Write below your own honest feeling about being called to take part in the ministry of evangelism.

_____

_____

Whether your feelings are negative or positive, attempt to explain why you feel this way.

_____

_____

2.   Make a list of reasons why working with others to build them in the faith is difficult.

    _____   _____

    _____   _____

    How can these difficulties best be overcome?

    _____

    _____

3.   If you have attempted to win people to Christ and they have declined your invitation to receive Him, what reasons did they give? Write an analysis of your witness, including strengths and weaknesses.

The Master and Your Plan—Step Three

Recently I visited one of the fastest growing churches in the United States. I have never been any more impressed by the combination of evangelistic outreach and apparent spiritual depth than I was with this congregation. The evolution of the program of evangelism in this church is interesting. Chronologically, it began when the pastor preached to his congregation that each of them should witness. This produced no witnesses. Then he held classes or study courses. The same result—no witnesses. Then the pastor began to take one man with him as he bore witness to Jesus. This man watched over a period of weeks as the pastor led people to Christ. Soon, the man got the idea and began to witness himself. He began to take a person with him and the pastor took another, so soon there were four. As people were won, they were trained to win others. The four became eight, the eight, sixteen, until now there are approximately five-hundred people in that church who can intelligently share their faith with others. It's no wonder that members of that church led to Christ over one thousand people last year! *They have learned the secret of multiplication.* They are following the Master's plan of evangelism.

Learning Procedures

1. The New Testament calls attention to a number of ways in which believers can be followed up. Listed below are four

Scripture verses. List the particular method of follow-up suggested by the verse.

(a) Acts 15:36 _____

(b) Philippians 1:9 _____

(c) 1 Thessalonians 3:1, 2 _____

(d) Galatians 6:11 _____

2. Nothing is more vital in follow-up ministry than prayer. Notice the content of two of Paul's prayers for believers which are recorded in Ephesians. List the particular requests he makes in their behalf.

(a) Ephesians 1:15–20

_____

_____

_____

_____

_____

(b) Ephesians 3:14–19

_____

_____

_____

_____

_____

Group Discussion and Activity

1. Discuss: What long-range goals are there in the organizational structure of our church which will help us incorporate the principles of the Master Plan? What short-range goals should we have for this year?

2. Brainstorming is a method of problem solving in which group members suggest in rapid-fire order all the possible solutions they can think of. Criticism is ruled out. Evaluation of ideas comes later.

Use the brainstorming method with the clause "variety and resourcefulness in a new and bold approach."

3. One of the paragraph headings in the last chapter is entitled "Methods Will Vary." Discuss a variety of methods which might be employed by either an individual or a small group.

4. If you are a part of outreach ministry to a convalescent home, jail, or detention home, discuss possible ways of leading those who make decisions to maturity.

Personal Achievement

1. If you have been working with a person, make suggestions to the person as to some people with whom he might begin to share his faith. Some of these would be:

_____

_____

_____

2. Here are some suggestions as to "How to have a quiet time." Share them with those with whom you have been working.

  (a) Have a definite time. Choose the most appropriate time for you individually.

  (b) Have a definite place. A place secluded from noise or interruptions is best. Be *alone* with God.

  (c) Have a definite plan in mind.
      First, make a list of requests for which to pray.
      Then, spend some of the time studying the Bible.

3. Undoubtedly, by now, you have had resistance from the enemy in your efforts to win and mature people. Those with whom you are working also experience this. Satan will tempt you and them along this line, "What do you mean trying to lead someone in the Christian life? You are too unworthy for this. You are not even sure of your own salvation." Learn to use the Word of God to meet his attacks. Meet this onslaught with I John 5:11–13.

  Next, he might whisper to you, "You may be a Christian,

all right, but look at the areas in which you have failed since becoming a Christian." Respond to this temptation with I John 1:9.

Third, he will tell you, that though you are a Christian, you are much too weak to resist temptation. On this occasion remember I Corinthians 10:13.

The Master and Your Plan—Step Four

The population of our world is increasing at an unbelievable rate. Every time a clock ticks off a second, world population has increased by two. This means there will be almost 200,000 more people in our world tomorrow than there are today, according to United Nations estimates. In one generation, if the trend continues, world population will exceed seven billion.

While the people-rate increases at the speed of a rocket, the rate at which these people are being reached with the Gospel virtually proceeds at the pace of an ox cart. The percentage of evangelical Christians in our world has grown smaller and smaller in recent decades. A famous evangelist has said, "We are not winning our world for Christ—we are losing our world for Christ." There is but one hope to stem the tide: *That is a return on the part of the church to the Master's plan of evangelism.*

What is the plan of your life, the one life God has entrusted to you? Are you investing it in a ministry which gives priority to working with people? Do you have your man or your small group in whom and through whom you are multiplying yourself? There are no worthwhile shortcuts in world evangelization. We must follow His plan, even at the price of being denied impressive statistical reports for the present. But with an eye to the future and a vision of His name proclaimed to every person, commit yourself anew to Jesus to do His work His way.

Learning Procedures

1. The New Testament describes new or immature Christians in terms of _____ .

2. What does the above term suggest as far as the need of follow-up is concerned? Check the following verses and list some needs of new or immature Christians.

   (a) Ephesians 4:14 _____

   (b) I Thessalonians 2:7, 11 _____

   (c) I Peter 2:2 _____

3. Paul and Barnabas spent approximately five months in the city of Thessalonica on his second missionary journey. Describe this church on the basis of I Thessalonians 1.

   _____

   _____

   How could this kind of church come from such a brief ministry?

   _____

   _____

4. We have been working toward leading believers to spiritual maturity. Listed below are verses which suggest some marks of a mature believer. List them.

   (a) II Corinthians 5:7 _____

   (b) I Thessalonians 5:18 _____

   (c) II Corinthians 9:7 _____

   (d) I John 3:16, 17 _____

   (e) Ephesians 6:18 _____

   (f) Hebrews 5:14 _____

Group Discussion and Activity

1. What small groups already exist in your church which could implement the principles of the Master Plan? List them on a blackboard.

2. With your books open to pages 115–126, let each one list in outline form the points considered essential for individuals to use if they are to disciple others. Discuss your findings.

3. Freely discuss difficulties you have had in witnessing and
    how they may be alleviated. Close with prayer for each
    other.

Personal Achievement

1. If you have had the privilege recently of leading someone to
    Christ, describe below in some detail your plans for helping
    to lead the person to spiritual maturity.

    _____

    _____

    _____

    _____

2. Briefly describe your plans for a permanent strategy of
    evangelism for your own life.

    _____

    _____

    _____

    _____

ANSWERS TO LEARNING PROCEDURES

(Page numbers referred to are from *The Master Plan of Evangelism*.)

Lesson 1
   3. Principles
   4. the Gospel records
   5. (a) F (b) F (c) F
Lesson 2
   1. (a) Judas (b) 500 (c) John
   2. (a) p. 21 (b) p. 21 (c) p. 23 (d) p. 24
   3. (a) F (b) F (c) T
Lesson 3
   2. (a) p. 38 (b) p. 39 (c) pp. 44, 45
   3. (a) more (b) ½ (c) the disciples
Lesson 4
   2. (b) p. 50 3. John 14:21 4. p. 58 6. B,D,A,E,C
Lesson 5
   1. p. 61 2. p. 63 3. p. 63 4. p. 66 5. pp. 62, 63 6. p. 61
Lesson 6
   1. pp. 73–77 2. p. 73 3. p. 76
Lesson 7
   1. p. 82 2. p. 83 3. p. 85 4. pp. 85, 86 5. p. 90 6. F, B, A, C, D, E
Lesson 8
   1. p. 95 2. p. 95 3. p. 96 4. p. 100
Lesson 9
   1. (a) F (b) T (c) T (d) T 3. p. 109 4. p. 110 5. p. 110 6. p. 112 7. p. 113
Lesson 10
   1. p. 118 2. p. 118 3. (a) p. 121 (b) p. 121 4. p. 124
Lesson 11
   1. assurance
      doctrinal stability
      Christlikeness
      winning others

discipling others
2. 4,294,967,296

Lesson 12
1. (a) personal contact
   (b) prayer
   (c) sending someone else
   (d) letters
Lesson 13
1. Babes
2. (a) protection from false doctrine
   (b) loving care and concern
   (c) food, the milk of the Word
4. (a) living by faith
   (b) giving thanks in everything
   (c) cheerful giving
   (d) compassion toward others
   (e) praying always
   (f) discernment

Bibliography

Allen, Roland. *Missionary Methods: St. Paul's or Ours?* Grand Rapids, Mich.: Wm. B. Eerdmans Publishing Co., 1962.
————. *Missionary Principles.* Grand Rapids, Mich.: Wm. B. Eerdmans Publishing Co., 1964.
————. *Spontaneous Expansion of the Church.* Grand Rapids, Mich.: Wm. B. Eerdmans Publishing Co., 1962.
Archibald, A. C. *Establishing the Convert.* Philadelphia, Pa.: Judson Press, 1952.
Augsburger, Myron S. *Invitation to Discipleship.* Scottdale, Pa.: Herald Press, 1964.
Bayly, Joseph. *The Gospel Blimp and Other Stories.* Grand Rapids, Mich.: Zondervan Publishing House.
Belew, M. Wendell. *Churches and How They Grow.* Nashville, Tenn.: Broadman Press, 1971.
Bender, Urie A. *The Witness.* Scottdale, Pa.: Herald Press, 1965.
Boer, Harry R. *Pentecost and Missions.* Grand Rapids, Mich.: Wm. B. Eerdmans Publishing Co.
Brooks, Hal. *Follow-up Evangelism.* Nashville, Tenn.: Broadman Press, 1972.
Brown, Stanley C. *Evangelism in the Early Church.* Grand Rapids, Mich.: Wm. B. Eerdmans Publishing Co., 1963.
Bruce, Alexander B. *The Training of the Twelve.* Grand Rapids, Mich.: Kregel Publications, 1979.
Call to Joy. Fort Worth, Tex.: International Evangelism Association, 1985.
Chafin, Kenneth L. *Help! I'm a Layman.* Waco, Tex.: Word Books, 1966.

Cho, Paul Yonggi, and Harold Hostetler. *Successful Home Cell Groups*. Plainfield, N.J.: Bridge Publishing Co., 1981.

Coggin, James E., and Bernard M. Spooner. *You Can Reach People Now*. Nashville, Tenn.: Broadman Press, 1971.

Coleman, Lyman. *Acts Alive, The Coffee House Itch, Dialogue, Groups in Action, Growth by Groups, Kaleidoscope, Man Alive*. Newton, Pa.: Halfway House.

Coleman, Robert E. *The Heartbeat of Evangelism*. Colorado Springs, Colo.: NavPress, 1985.

―――. *The Master Plan of Evangelism*. Old Tappan, N.J.: Fleming H. Revell Co., 1964.

Cosgrove, Francis M. *Essentials of Discipleship*. Colorado Springs, Colo.: NavPress, 1980.

―――. *Essentials of New Life*. Colorado Springs, Colo.: NavPress, 1978.

Cotteril, J. Hills and M. Heines. *Know How to Lead Bible Study and Discussion Groups*. London: Scripture Union.

Dawson, Dave. *Equipping the Saints*. Equipping the Saints, 1984.

Derham, A. Morgan. *A Christian's Guide to Bible Study*. London: Hodder and Stoughton, Ltd.

Discipleship Coordination Handbook. Fort Worth, Tex.: International Evangelism Association, 1983.

Douglas, M. R. *How to Build an Evangelistic Church*. Grand Rapids, Mich.: Zondervan Publishing House.

Eims, Leroy. *Be the Leader You Were Meant to Be*. Wheaton, Ill.: Victor Books, 1975.

―――. *Disciples in Action*. Wheaton, Ill.: Victor Books, 1981.

―――. *Laboring in the Harvest*. Colorado Springs, Colo.: NavPress, 1985.

―――. *The Lost Art of Disciple Making*. Colorado Springs, Colo.: NavPress, 1978.

―――. *What Every Christian Should Know About Growing*. Wheaton, Ill.: Victor Books, 1976.

Fish, Roy J., and J. H. Conant. *Every Member Evangelism for Today*. New York: Harper and Row, Publishers, 1976.

Fleischmann, Paul, ed. *Discipling the Young Person*. San Bernardino, Calif.: Here's Life Publishers, Inc., 1985.

Ford, Leighton. *The Christian Persuader*. New York: Harper and Row, Publishers, 1966.

Foster, Robert D. *The Navigator.* Colorado Springs, Colo.: NavPress, 1983.

Greenhough, J. G. *The Apostles of Our Lord.* London: Hodder and Stoughton, Ltd., 1904.

Hadidian, Allen. *Successful Discipling.* Chicago, Ill.: Moody Press, 1979.

Hanks, Billie. *If You Love Me.* Waco, Tex.: Word Books, 1985.

———. *My Spiritual Notebook.* Waco, Tex.: Word Books, 1977.

Hanks, Billie, Jr., and William A. Shell. *Discipleship: The Best Writings of the Most Experienced Disciple Makers.* Grand Rapids, Mich.: Zondervan Publishing House, 1981.

———. *Everyday Evangelism.* Grand Rapids, Mich.: Zondervan Publishing House, 1981.

Hanks, Billie, Jr., and Billy Beacham. *Spiritual Journal.* Waco, Tex.: Word Books, 1981.

Hartman, Doug, and Doug Sutherland. *A Guidebook to Discipleship.* Irvine, Calif.: Harvest House, 1976.

Hendrix, John, and Lloyd Householder, eds. *The Equipping of Disciples.* Nashville, Tenn.: Broadman Press, 1977.

Henrichsen, Walter A. *Disciples Are Made—Not Born.* Wheaton, Ill.: Victor Books, 1974.

———. *How to Disciple Your Children.* Wheaton, Ill.: Victor Books, 1981.

Henry, Carl F. H., and W. Stanley Mooneyham, eds. *One Race, One Gospel, One Task.* Vol. 1 and Vol. 2. Minneapolis, Minn.: World Wide Publications, 1962.

Hull, Bill. *Jesus Christ Disciplemaker.* Colorado Springs, Colo.: NavPress, 1984.

Kennedy, D. James. *Evangelism Explosion.* Wheaton, Ill.: Tyndale House Publishers, 1970.

Kraemer, Hendrik. *A Theology of the Laity.* London: Lutterworth Press.

Kuhne, Gary W. *The Dynamics of Discipleship Training.* Grand Rapids, Mich.: Zondervan Publishing House, 1977.

———. *The Dynamics of Personal Follow-up.* Grand Rapids, Mich.: Zondervan Publishing House, 1976.

Kunz, Marilyn, and Catherine Schell. *How to Start a Neighborhood Bible Study.* Wheaton, Ill.: Tyndale House Publishers, 1970.

Larson, Bruce. *Living on the Growing Edge*. Grand Rapids, Mich.: Zondervan Publishing House, 1968.

———. *Setting Men Free*. Grand Rapids, Mich.: Zondervan Publishing House, 1967.

Latham, Henry. *Pastor Pastorum*. Cambridge: Deighton Bell & Co., 1910.

Little, Paul E. *How to Give Away Your Faith*. Downers Grove, Ill.: InterVarsity Press, 1966.

MacDonald, William. *True Discipleship*. Fort Dodge, Iowa: Walterick Publishers, 1962.

MacKay, W. MacKintosh. *The Men Whom Jesus Made*. New York: George Doran Company, 1924.

Miller, Paul. *Group Dynamics in Evangelism*. Scottdale, Pa.: Herald Press, 1958.

Moore, Wayland B. *New Testament Follow-Up*. Grand Rapids, Mich.: Wm. B. Eerdmans Publishing Co., 1963.

Moore, Waylon B. *Multiplying Disciples*. Colorado Springs, Colo.: Mission Unlimited, 1981.

Nyquist, James F., and Jack Kuhatschek. *Leading Bible Discussions*. Downers Grove, Ill.: InterVarsity Press, 1985.

Ortiz, Juan Carlos. *Call to Discipleship*. Plainfield, N.J.: Logos, 1975.

———. *The Disciple*. Wheaton, Ill.: Creation House, 1975.

Paul/Timothy Follow-Up Packet. Fort Worth, Tex.: International Evangelism Association, 1986.

Peace, Richard. *Witness*. Grand Rapids, Mich.: Zondervan Publishing House, 1971.

Pentecost, J. Dwight. *Design for Discipleship*. Grand Rapids, Mich.: Zondervan Publishing House, 1977.

Petersen, Jim. *Evangelism as a Lifestyle*. Colorado Springs, Colo.: NavPress, 1980.

Powell, Paul W. *Dynamic Discipleship*. Nashville, Tenn.: Broadman Press, 1984.

Powell, S. W. *Where Are the Converts?* Nashville, Tenn.: Broadman Press, 1958.

Price, J. M. *Jesus the Teacher*. Nashville, Tenn.: Convention Press, 1946.

Rinker, Rosalind. *Communicating Love Through Prayer*. Grand Rapids, Mich.: Zondervan Publishing House, 1966.

————. *Prayer: Conversing With God*. Grand Rapids, Mich.: Zondervan Publishing House, n.d.

————. *Praying Together*. Grand Rapids, Mich.: Zondervan Publishing House, 1968.

————. *You Can Witness With Confidence*. Grand Rapids, Mich.: Zondervan Publishing House, 1984.

Sanny, Lorne. *The Art of Personal Witnessing*. Chicago, Ill.: Moody Press, 1957.

————. *Marks of a Disciple*. Colorado Springs, Colo.: NavPress, 1975.

Seamands, John T. *On Tiptoe with Joy!* Kansas City, Mo.: Beacon Hill Press, 1967.

Shoemaker, Samuel Moore, ed. *Groups That Work*. Grand Rapids, Mich.: Zondervan Publishing House, n.d.

Skinner, Betty Lee. *Daws*. Grand Rapids, Mich.: Zondervan Publishing House, 1974.

Smith, Asbury. *The Twelve Christ Chose*. New York: Harper and Row, Publishers, 1958.

Smith, Hannah Whitall. *The Christian's Secret of a Happy Life*. Westwood, N.J.: Fleming H. Revell Company, 1966.

Smith, J. Edgar. *Friendship Evangelism*. Anderson, Ind.: Warner Press, Inc.

Stott, John R. *Basic Christianity*. Grand Rapids, Mich.: Wm. B. Eerdmans Publishing Co., 1957.

————. *Our Guilty Silence*. Grand Rapids, Mich.: Wm. B. Eerdmans Publishing Co., 1969.

Taylor, Jack R. *The Key to Triumphant Living*. Nashville, Tenn.: Broadman Press, 1978.

Thomas, Ian. *The Saving Life of Christ*. Grand Rapids, Mich.: Zondervan Publishing House, 1961.

Thompson, W. Oscar, Jr., and Carolyn Thompson. *Concentric Circles of Concern*. Nashville, Tenn.: Broadman Press, 1981.

Toyotome, Masumi. *The Manual of the Nameless Movement*. Manila, Philippines: Christian Literature Crusade, 1968.

Trotman, Dawson E. *Born to Reproduce*. Colorado Springs, Colo.: The Navigators, 1955.

————. *Born to Reproduce* (booklet). Colorado Springs, Colo.: NavPress, 1975.

Trueblood, Elton. *The Company of the Committed*. New York: Harper and Row, Publishers, 1980.

————. *The Incendiary Fellowship.* New York: Harper and Row, Publishers, 1961.

Warr, Gene. *The Godly Man.* Creative Resources, 1976.

————. *You Can Make Disciples.* Waco, Tex.: Word Books, 1978.

Warr, Irma. *The Godly Woman.* Creative Resources, 1976.

Warren, Richard. *Twelve Dynamic Bible Study Methods.* Wheaton, Ill.: Victor, 1981.

Webster, Douglas. *What Is Evangelism?* London: The Highway Press, n.d.

Wilson, Carl. *With Christ in the School of Disciple Building.* Grand Rapids, Mich.: Zondervan Publishing House, 1976.

Wood, Barry, *Questions New Christians Ask.* Old Tappan, N.J.: Fleming H. Revell, 1979.